MW00561686

12 New Testament Passages That Changed the World

Joseph Bentz

THE FOUNDRY
PUBLISHING

978-0-8341-3817-9

Printed in the
United States of America

Cover design: J.R. Caines
Interior design: Sharon Page

Library of Congress Cataloging-in-Publication Data
Names: Bentz, Joseph, 1961- author.
Title: 12 New Testament passages that changed the world / Joseph Bentz.
Description: Kansas City : The Foundry Publishing, 2019. | Includes bibliographical references. | Summary: "In 12 New Testament Passages That Changed the World, author Joseph Bentz explores some of the most life-changing New Testament scriptures and demonstrates their ability to touch all types of people, even those who don't believe in Jesus"—Provided by publisher.
Identifiers: LCCN 2019026127 (print) | LCCN 2019026128 (ebook) | ISBN 9780834138179 (paperback) | ISBN 9780834138186 (ebook)
Subjects: LCSH: Bible. New Testament—Criticism, interpretation, etc. | Bible. New Testament—Influence.
Classification: LCC BS2361.3 .B46 2019 (print) | LCC BS2361.3 (ebook) | DDC 225.6—dc23
LC record available at https://lccn.loc.gov/2019026127
LC ebook record available at https://lccn.loc.gov/2019026128

Interior photos provided by Bridgeman Images (chapters 2, 3, 4, 5, 6), Art Resource (chapters 1, 7, 8, 9, 10, 11, 12), and Shutterstock (chapters 13, 14).

The internet addresses, email addresses, and phone numbers in this book are accurate at the time of publication. They are provided as a resource. The Foundry Publishing does not endorse them or vouch for their content or permanence.

10 9 8 7 6 5 4 3 2 1

Contents

1

Gutenberg Bible // Johann Gutenberg and Johann Fust // c. 1455

Does the Bible
Still Matter?

IS THE BIBLE'S RELEVANCE fading in our secular age? Or is it becoming increasingly more widespread and influential across the globe as new technologies spread it to places that have never seen it, in forms that no one could have imagined even a few decades ago?

I recently came across two articles published on the same day. The first was an interview with Kenneth A. Briggs, author of a new book about the Bible's waning influence in public life. He said that "people aren't reading [the Bible] very much, and it just doesn't show up in—as they love to say—public discourse. It doesn't really make many appearances, and it is not in the public consciousness. The Bible is off the grid in a way I've never experienced before."[1]

A few hours later I came across a very different story about the Bible's influence on today's culture worldwide. It reported that the YouVersion Bible app has now reached more than 250 million downloads across the globe. That's a quarter of a billion people accessing the Bible on a technology that didn't even exist a few short years ago. Of course, it's one thing to download an app, but are these people really *reading* the Bible on it? The study showed that in the year 2016 alone, users read and listened to more than 13 billion chapters, created more than a billion highlights, bookmarks, and notes, and shared verses a record 230 million times.[2]

Those astonishing statistics show that the Bible still exerts a powerful influence on millions—if not billions—of people. The good news is that the Bible is easier and cheaper than ever to access and read. It's as close as your nearest electronic device, and for most people, it's probably pretty close by on a bookshelf or nightstand too.

Yet Briggs's research on the Bible's diminishing visibility in certain areas of life should not be lightly dismissed. Even for Christians who revere the Bible, it's hard to deny that it is easier to think or say nice things *about* the Bible than it is to dig into it in a serious way. And, just because verses get posted (out of context) millions of times on social media and elsewhere, that doesn't mean people truly understand what they're posting. The Bible is abused as much as it is used, and large swaths of the population have only vague—and often wrong—ideas about its contents.

In one sense, even people who are hostile to the Bible cannot escape its influence. The book has simply shaped too much of life for people to completely dismiss it. Maybe you have never read a word from a Bible—yet you probably still know what a "good Samaritan" is or what people mean when they call someone a "prodigal son." You've probably heard of the Golden Rule. When you see a cross on a chain around someone's neck, you probably know that the cross represents the device on which Jesus Christ was crucified.

Even readers who are hostile to Christianity still usually recognize which particular prayer The Lord's Prayer refers to, and they may even be able to quote it from memory, whether they want to or not. The Last Supper may not have any significance to them as far as what they believe or how they live, but they still probably know it was the final meal Jesus had with his disciples on the night before he was executed. Their knowledge of that meal may derive more directly from Leonardo da Vinci's famous painting than from the Bible itself, but that only highlights the Bible's wide-ranging influence across centuries and in every area of life. It is hard to think of an area of life—art, music, law, film, literature, medicine, and many others—that has not been deeply influenced by the Bible.

Wycliffe Bible Translators USA reported a few years ago that 5.8 billion people now have access to all or some of the Bible translated in their first language.[3] The complete Bible has been translated into 683 languages, and the New Testament has been translated into at least 1,534 languages.[4]

What Is It about This Book?

What is it about the Bible that makes it so influential? How have certain key portions of Scripture managed to shift civilizations and transform individual lives? The purpose of my book is to celebrate and explore some of the twelve most important passages of the New Testament in order to probe why they are so powerful. This book will focus on the New Testament, and another book is planned to delve into the Old Testament.

Some readers may have only a surface knowledge of these New Testament passages, and this book may open a window into their beauty and power. Other readers may be very familiar with the passages, but perhaps overfamiliarity has caused them to grow a little cold. This book may bring them back to life or shed new light on passages readers thought they already knew.

Sometimes the most famous portions of Scripture are also the most abused or misunderstood, such as "Judge not," or, "All things work together for the good . . ." This book will consider the passages in their original context while also showing the impact they have had on the world. The history of the Bible shows how amazing it is that this book came together in the first place and that it went on to become the bestselling book of all time. The Holy Spirit has powerfully used these words to draw people to him across generations and cultures, and the work the Spirit is doing with this book is still not finished.

After reading the interview with Briggs about the waning influence of the Bible in public life, I got a copy of his book to see what else he had to say. His focus is on the Bible's influence in the United States rather than the world as a whole, and he identifies a number of forces that gradually eroded the Bible's importance, such as scholarship that challenged aspects of authorship and other elements of the Bible, scientific theories that offered views other than the Bible's about how the world came about, and biblical teaching that challenged America's love of individualism.

The public education system also is not inclined to promote biblical literacy. Taking the Bible seriously means believing in the supernatural and in God's revelation rather than believing only in science or materialism, and where in the curriculum does the supernatural fit? Public schools and universities may allow for study of the Bible as a literary document or a work that has influenced Western civilization, but these educational institutions do not embrace it as a sacred text.[5]

Even when people do believe the Bible, how seriously do they take it? Briggs says many churches have downplayed the Bible in their worship services as congregations have become less familiar with it, which only feeds biblical illiteracy. And even though the nation is awash in Bibles—the Gideons alone have distributed more than two billion of them since 1908, and American homes own an average of four or five Bibles each—fewer people are actually reading it, just as they are reading fewer long books on any topic. Briggs quotes Philip Towner, head of the American Bible Society's research institute, who said, "It's not the age of Bible reading anymore; it's the age of Bible buying."[6] That is certainly a bleak picture, but is it the entire picture?

Imagine This

Imagine a scenario in which all those billions of Bibles were suddenly taken away from everyone and destroyed. No more Bibles on paper, no Bible apps, no tens of thousands of editions in a few thousand languages. This limitless selection of Bible editions is replaced by one edition—but there is a catch. Only churches, not individuals, will be issued this new edition, and each church will receive no more than one, and that one will be only for ministers to use. Oh, and there is one other catch: the edition will be translated only into an obscure language that few people know.

Do you think that would spell doom for the Bible's influence in public and private life? Keeping the Bible out of people's hands and letting them hear it read in church only, in a language most of them won't know, may sound like the perfect way to snuff out the book altogether, but for most of the history of Christianity, up until the last five hundred years or so, that was mainly the way everyday Christians experienced it.

Let's say you're a rank-and-file Christian layperson in the year 1300 somewhere in England. You almost certainly would not have your own copy of the Bible. Why? For one thing, each copy of the Bible would have to be copied and produced by hand. The Bible is a *long* book, so such copies would be both expensive and rare. Not that it would do you much good to have a copy even if you could obtain one because the translation would be in Latin, a language you probably would not know. Only a relatively small number of men—and they would almost certainly be men—would know that language.

As if the Latin and the lack of literacy among most of the population and the scarcity of books were not enough obstacles to overcome, the church didn't want you reading the Bible on your own anyway. The Bible was not for individual use. Better to let the church present it to you, they thought, and interpret it for you, than to risk what might happen if this powerful book were placed into the hands of individual readers.

Did those confining circumstances prevent Christians from knowing and believing in the Bible? No. As Bible historian Lori Anne Ferrell puts it, "Lively participants in a scripture-saturated culture, the vast majority of medieval folk were both illiterate *and* deeply familiar with Holy Writ."[7] How is that possible? Ferrell explains that these laypeople would have heard the Latin Vulgate Bible spoken aloud in their churches their whole lives. The repetition of the Latin phrases "would have coalesced into a composite language, comprehensible to audiences destined never to read nor to write Latin, transforming what should have been gibberish into the practice of piety. As a vernacular religious treatise from 1375 stated, even 'when not understood, the power of God's word still avails.'"[8]

The power of God's word still avails. In other words, in spite of all the barriers to biblical understanding, the Bible not only survived in that era, but its words and message also sank deeply into people's souls. The Holy Spirit brought

Scripture to life even in people who were mostly illiterate and hearing God's Word in a strange language.

Experiencing the Bible in Community

The work of the Holy Spirit in keeping Scripture alive during the pre-printing press, pre-Reformation, pre-King James Version era of Christianity gives me hope for our day. Experiencing the Bible then was a communal event. People gathered in churches to hear the Word. They also created art that portrayed biblical scenes. They listened to sermons in their own language that expounded on Scripture.

Another method that emerged to bring the Bible into people's awareness during the medieval period were mystery plays that depicted Bible stories. These cycles of plays were performed on moving stages that rolled through town as people waited for the next one to come to them. Entire towns got involved in these performances, as either performers or spectators. They brought the Bible to life for people who could not read it. As Ferrell describes it, "The audience staked out places along the streets; the plays came to them, one after another, unfolding in unrelenting narrative sequence. A full biblical cycle could comprise as many as twenty-four plays, from the Fall of Lucifer to the Last Judgment, and could last many hours—or up to three days."[9] These plays were performed during festivals such as the Feast of Corpus Christi, when people took off work and mixed their Bible dramas with celebration and drinking and rowdiness. The plays were not always accurate in the details of Scripture, and they represented not only biblical narrative but also the theological bents of the playwrights who crafted them. But as a whole, they are an example of one of the ways Christians of that era learned, studied, and even performed the Bible in community.

Although I am grateful that I now have numerous biblical translations in my own language to choose from, I am also thankful that the Bible has never needed ideal conditions in order to thrive. And, while today my most common way of interacting with Scripture is reading a Bible on my own (plus encountering it in smaller segments in sermons and Sunday school classes), reading it on my own was not how I first learned it. My first encounters with Scripture remind me more of a medieval Christian's experience than that of a twenty-first-century believer. I was a child, brought to Sunday school classes and Vacation Bible Schools. I couldn't simply sit down and read the Bible on my own. It was too long and complex.

Instead, I first heard the stories told by loving, patient Sunday school teachers, who brought the stories to life in colorful books, flannel graph displays, coloring books, and songs. Through those lessons I learned about Jesus healing the sick, Paul encountering Jesus on the road to Damascus, Noah building his ark, Moses receiving the Ten Commandments, and many other stories. In Vacation Bible School we made little crafts out of paper towel rolls, bars of soap, paint, crayons, egg cartons, and popsicle sticks to help us envision the stories in concrete ways. All these methods were fun, but looking back, I can see that the Holy Spirit was also using all this singing and painting and storytelling and creating to prepare me to understand the Bible and to know Jesus. When I was ready, I approached the Bible the old-fashioned way: I started to read it.

Even then, I didn't simply start from the beginning and read it straight through. Instead, my community of fellow Christians guided me toward key passages first. In fourth grade we memorized John 3:16, 1 John 1:9, and other important verses. As a teenager I was involved in Bible quizzing, where we learned and memorized large portions of New Testament books and made a friendly competition out of it. Later I did read the whole Bible for myself, took biblical literature and theology courses, and learned from Bible scholars and other Christian writers. Through all of this I had advantages the medieval Christians did not, but like them, my encounters with the Bible—even the reading I did "on my own"—was guided by my faith community.

I picked the medieval era as an example of a time when the Bible thrived in spite of unfavorable conditions, but I could have chosen almost any era of Christian history. Each had its own challenges. Although the medieval Bible audience struggled with illiteracy, church control, translation problems, printing problems, and so on, at least those periods had an actual text of the Bible to work with. Before that, it was amazing that the Bible as we now know it came together at all. If you travel back in time about a thousand years before the situation that existed in the year 1300, in what condition would you find the Bible and its readers at that point?

Ferrell describes a disorganized and far-flung group of Christians, some facing persecution from the Roman Empire, who had widely varying ideas of what Scripture even *was*: "Some assemblies used nothing but the Greek version of the Hebrew Bible; some believed in nothing but the Gospels and rejected the Jewish scriptures of a common past; still others revered writings that told stories of Jesus that challenged doctrines espoused by church leaders, who issued directives from places safely far away: Rome, Milan, Jerusalem."[10] Over the course of generations to come, the canon of Scripture was finally formed (though even now there are different versions of it), but centuries more would pass before most Christians would hold their own copies of the Bible and read it in their own language.

Drowning in Bibles

Christians of earlier eras had to be creative to experience Scripture, and some cultures throughout the world still struggle with laws against the Bible or other barriers that keep people from it. But in the United States and many other nations, the only problem is deciding which of the endless versions and styles of the Bible to choose from. A quick online search led me to such versions as the Life Application Study Bible, The Message, The Woman's Bible, Inspire Bible NLT: The Bible for Creative Journaling (with wide margins and line drawings in some margins for coloring and journaling), the ESV Global Study Bible, the Teen Life Application Study Bible NLT, the NIV Gift Bible (in pink or chocolate color), The Action Bible, The Story Bible (for new believers, with boring parts left out and stories emphasized), the NIV Boys Bible, The Everyday Life Bible, the NIV Bible for Teen Girls, the Every Man's Bible NLT, the Deluxe Explorer Edition, and many others.

Each demographic—children, women, men, and teenagers—has multiple Bible options to select from. There are also large-print Bibles, tiny Bibles, pocket Bibles, leather-bound editions, embossed Bibles, red-letter editions (with Jesus's words in red), and many other choices. If that is not enough, you can find plenty of Bible accessories, such as a highlighter kit, a wide variety of decorative covers, Bible stands, Bible verse cell phone cases, Bible jewelry, and a Bible Taboo board game.

It's easy to make fun of many of these products, and sometimes the mockery is deserved. This profusion of Bible products also shows that, among other things, the Bible is a commodity to market and sell. There are plenty of examples of commercial exploitation of Scripture. On the other hand, all these versions and supplies also show the intense interest people have not only in possessing this book but also, perhaps, in making sense of it and making it part of one's life. The Bible is a daunting book, so maybe products like highlighter kits and decorative covers and devotional aids help make it more approachable for some readers.

Many Christians lament the fact that we no longer live in one of the Bible-saturated eras of days gone by, when scriptural references and stories were as well known to people as stories about celebrities or the Super Bowl or other pop culture phenomena. However, for every statistic or anecdote that indicates the Bible's influence is waning, I seem to run across just as many examples of Scripture reaching people in ways never before possible throughout history. Some of this is thanks to new technology, like the YouVersion Bible app mentioned earlier. Social media platforms of all kinds have also spread Bible verses and Bible studies and Bible commentaries around the globe. On Twitter alone, more than 40 million tweets about Bible verses went out in a single year. About half of those were sent out by bot accounts that do nothing but pump out Bible verses nonstop.[11]

The Bible is also being translated into new languages in ways that were not possible in earlier eras. One difficulty with Bible translation has been that some cultures do not have a written alphabet. Translators would therefore have to create an alphabet and a written language and then teach it to the speakers of that language before the Bible could be translated. A new software called Render is being developed that will skip the written translation and instead translate the Bible orally. A translator who knows the local language and also a nearby major language into which the Bible has already been translated can record a new, spoken translation. Robin Green, project manager at Faith Comes by Hearing, said, "Render means that some languages that might have fallen through the cracks will get Scripture."[12]

Even as new technology brings the Bible to life on tiny screens around the world, another Bible publisher is moving in the opposite direction, finding ways to enhance a more traditional way of approaching the Bible in book form. Crossway, which publishes the English Standard Version (ESV) Bible, has created a six-volume edition that emphasizes the beauty of the physical book itself and that tries to make the reading experience more inviting. Because the Bible is so long, publishers have struggled to print it in ways that make it easily readable. Cramming it into one volume often leads to smaller print, cramped lines, and flimsy paper. Many readers may not give much thought to such issues, but in the long run, those problems can push people away from Scripture just because the reading process itself becomes such a strain. Readers might feel compelled to put the book down even if they don't consciously identify *why* they feel that way.

The editors of the six-volume set counter those reading difficulties with careful attention to every detail of the reading experience. Breaking the Bible into six volumes allows them to use thicker paper, which makes the text on the page cleaner, sharper, and brighter. Pages are less cluttered and look more like a high-quality hardcover novel. Covers come in cloth or leather and feel good in your hands. The binding of each volume makes the book easy to hold open, with the pages not flipping back as you read. In a video created to describe the details of the new edition, one of the editors explains that the intent was to "create a Bible with such beauty and quality and excellence that honors and reflects the beauty of the content that's within."[13]

The Bible sets are expensive and won't be practical for every reader, but I love the idea of creating a version of the Bible that can draw readers in, slow them down, and encourage them to become immersed in the text the same way many of us do with a new book by a favorite author. In fact, I am in favor of any move that brings people into closer contact with Scripture. We live in a world that is drowning in Bibles, both online and on paper, but ironically, the book has become easier than ever to ignore. If we're not ignoring it, we are often mistreating it. We proof-text verses to serve our purposes rather than allowing the words to change us. We use verses the way we use memes on social media—a saying or two here or there to represent our feeling at the moment. If that's all the Bible is to us, then we are even worse off than people centuries ago, who didn't have their own copies of the Bible but who still took it seriously enough to learn it through whatever means were available to them.

No matter how familiar you may think you are with the Bible, familiarity is no guarantee that the Bible will stay alive within you. The following chapters will shine a fresh light on some of the most influential portions of the New Testament. How have these words changed the world? Why are they so powerful? What significance can they have in our lives today? My hope and prayer is that your understanding of Scripture will be deepened—or even shaken up— as much as my own has been as I have examined the vast influence of these passages. I hope that, by the time you reach the end of this book, you will love and appreciate the Bible more than you ever have before. May the power of God's Word still avail!

Notes

1. Emily McFarlan Miller, "Veteran Religion Reporter Looks for the Bible in Public Life in New Book," *The Colorado Springs Gazette*, December 11, 2016, https://gazette.com/life /veteran-religion-reporter-looks-for-the-bible-in-public-life/article_bf6da994-7d70-517f-811c -a5ca1ed32bb2.html.

2. "YouVersion Bible Downloads Milestone," CBA: The Association for Christian Retail, n.d., http://cbaonline.org/youversion-bible-downloads-milestone/.

3. "Wycliffe Reports 5.8 Billion People Now Have Access to Bible," *The Christian Post*, November 11, 2014. https://www.christianpost.com/news/wycliffe-reaches-5-8-billion-people -with-bible-translations-129536/.

4. "Scripture and Language Statistics 2018," Wycliffe Global Alliance, October 2018, http://www.wycliffe.net/en/statistics.

5. Kenneth A. Briggs, *The Invisible Bestseller: Searching for the Bible in America* (Grand Rapids: William B. Eerdmans Publishing Company, 2016), 2, 38.

6. Briggs, *The Invisible Bestseller*, 1, 5.

7. Lori Anne Ferrell, *The Bible and the People* (New Haven: Yale University Press, 2008), 28.

8. Ferrell, *The Bible and the People*, 28.

9. Ferrell, *The Bible and the People*, 47.

10. Ferrell, *The Bible and the People*, 7.

11. Meredith Gould, Pauline Hope Cheong, Rachel Barach, Phil Cooke, and Frank Thielman, "Spamming the Good News," *Christianity Today* 60, no. 5:23, 2016.

12. Sarah Eekhoff Zylstra, "Mouth to Mouth," *Christianity Today* 60, no. 4:18, 2016.

13. Don Jones, in "Introducing the 'ESV Reader's Bible, Six-Volume Set,'" Crossway, https://www.youtube.com/watch?v=ydtxcJxdmX0.

Digging Deeper

1. This chapter presents evidence that the influence of the Bible is diminishing in our day, and it presents other evidence that the Bible's reach and influence are increasing. What evidence on either side of this question did you find most worrisome, and what did you find most hopeful?

2. Reflect on your own experience with the Bible. How significant a role does it play in your life, if any? What role would you like it to play in the future?

3. This chapter sheds light on various ways that people throughout history have experienced the Bible—through plays, in church communities, in sermons, in art, and other ways. In addition to reading the Bible for yourself, can you think of any other ways you have experienced it that have been particularly memorable or meaningful?

4. This chapter shows many obstacles that threatened to keep the Bible from readers over the centuries, including illiteracy, church control, language barriers, technological limitations, and other barriers. What forces do you see that counteracted those difficulties and allowed the Bible to become perhaps the most influential book of all time?

5. What do you envision for the future of the Bible? Do you believe new technologies and new ways of presenting the Bible will increase its readership? Will apathy or hostility counteract those advances? Will the Holy Spirit continue to cause God's Word to avail in spite of everything?

Go to https://www.thefoundrypublishing.com/12NT/LeaderGuide for a free downloadable leader's guide that includes more questions for reflection as well as activities for use in a small group setting.

Jesus's Best Stories

2

The Return of the Prodigal Son // Rembrandt // c. 1668

The Prodigal Son

[11] *Jesus continued: "There was a man who had two sons.* [12] *The younger one said to his father, 'Father, give me my share of the estate.' So he divided his property between them.*

[13] *"Not long after that, the younger son got together all he had, set off for a distant country and there squandered his wealth in wild living.* [14] *After he had spent everything, there was a severe famine in that whole country, and he began to be in need.* [15] *So he went and hired himself out to a citizen of that country, who sent him to his fields to feed pigs.* [16] *He longed to fill his stomach with the pods that the pigs were eating, but no one gave him anything.*

[17] *"When he came to his senses, he said, 'How many of my father's hired servants have food to spare, and here I am starving to death!* [18] *I will set out and go back to my father and say to him: Father, I have sinned against heaven and against you.* [19] *I am no longer worthy to be called your son; make me like one of your hired servants.'* [20] *So he got up and went to his father.*

"But while he was still a long way off, his father saw him and was filled with compassion for him; he ran to his son, threw his arms around him and kissed him.

[21] *"The son said to him, 'Father, I have sinned against heaven and against you. I am no longer worthy to be called your son.'*

[22] *"But the father said to his servants, 'Quick! Bring the best robe and put it on him. Put a ring on his finger and sandals on his feet.* [23] *Bring the fattened calf and kill it. Let's have a feast and celebrate.* [24] *For this son of mine was dead and is alive again; he was lost and is found.' So they began to celebrate.*

[25] *"Meanwhile, the older son was in the field. When he came near the house, he heard music and dancing.* [26] *So he called one of the servants and asked him what was going on.* [27] *'Your brother has come,' he replied, 'and your father has killed the fattened calf because he has him back safe and sound.'*

[28] *"The older brother became angry and refused to go in. So his father went out and pleaded with him.* [29] *But he answered his father, 'Look! All these years I've been slaving for you and never disobeyed your orders. Yet you never gave me even a young goat so I could celebrate with my friends.* [30] *But when this son of yours who has squandered your property with prostitutes comes home, you kill the fattened calf for him!'*

[31] *"'My son,' the father said, 'you are always with me, and everything I have is yours.* [32] *But we had to celebrate and be glad, because this brother of yours was dead and is alive again; he was lost and is found.'"*

—*Luke 15: 11–32*

ONE CLUE that a fictional character has become truly influential in a culture is when that character is known by people who have never read or seen the novels or films in which the character first appeared. Many people know who Sherlock Holmes is even if they have never read a word of Sir Arthur Conan Doyle's stories about him. The fame of Mickey Mouse goes far beyond any particular cartoon in which he has appeared. People know of Harry Potter or Darth Vader even if they have never read the *Harry Potter* books or watched the *Star Wars* films. Some characters, like Santa Claus or Barbie, did not even originate in a particular text but still have cultural influence worldwide.

The prodigal son is a two-thousand-year-old character almost everyone has heard of even if they have never read Jesus's parable about him (the text of which does not, by the way, include the term "prodigal"). Ask someone to identify a prodigal in their family, and they can almost always do it. Sometimes it's themselves. The rebellious one. The one who strayed. Maybe they refer to the one who strayed and then returned.

The story of the prodigal son is so vivid in most people's imaginations that we don't even need full sentences to capture its essence. A few simple phrases provide the essential outline: Rebel son flees from home. Seeks faraway pleasures. Squanders resources. Hits rock bottom. Embarrassment. Shame. Plans a negotiated return. Servant? Trepidation. Turns toward home. Father sees from afar, runs, embraces. Fatted calf. Ring. Party. Forgiveness. Restoration. Nearby, outside the party, a brother broods.

That's the story as it flashes through my mind, and those vivid themes show why it's one of my favorite stories that Jesus tells. Restoration. Hope. Forgiveness. Unconditional love.

You may have noticed that little sour note at the end, the bitter older brother. He often gets downplayed when people think of this story, but he's important. We'll get back to him shortly. But when people tell and retell this story, as they have countless times over the centuries in paintings, films, novels, songs, even ballets, the younger, more openly rebellious brother is the one who gets most of the attention. Some artists try to retell the whole story, but many focus on one strand of it, such as sibling rivalry, or rebellion against fathers, or the pain, joy, or drama of coming home.

Rembrandt treated the story directly in his beloved painting *The Return of the Prodigal Son*, which shows the repentant son, in ragged and dirty clothes, kneeling before his father and burying his face in his father's chest. The father leans over him, hands lovingly placed on his shoulders, as others look on. Henri Nouwen, who first saw a poster of the painting pinned to a friend's office door, was so moved by it that he eventually wrote a book about this painting's impact on him.

In 1986 Nouwen got the opportunity to go to the Soviet Union and see Rembrandt's painting at the Hermitage in Saint Petersburg. An art expert friend made arrangements for him not only to see the painting but to spend hours gazing at it and reflecting on it. In his book he writes that, as time went on, he began to see the painting "as, somehow, my personal painting, the painting that contained not only the heart of the story that God wants to tell me, but also the heart of the story that I want to tell to God and God's people. All of the gospel is there. All of my life is there. . . . The painting has become a mysterious window through which I can step into the kingdom of God."[1]

Rembrandt powerfully captures a scene from the parable in his painting, but artists in other fields, such as music, dance, and literature, have also offered their own retellings of the story. George Balanchine's ballet *The Prodigal Son* (*Le Fils prodigue*), for example, emphasizes the son's seduction by the beautiful woman who robs him and helps bring about his downfall before he flees home to the father.

Some retellings of the parable not only borrow from Jesus's story but can also enhance the reader's understanding of it. Norman Maclean's novel *A River Runs Through It*, for example—which was later made into a popular film of the same name starring Brad Pitt, Craig Sheffer, and Tom Skerritt—contains echoes of the parable that heighten the truth of both stories. *A River Runs Through It* is set in Montana in the 1920s. It tells the story of a father who is a Presbyterian minister and his two sons, Norman and Paul, the older of whom is responsible and steady and the younger of whom is reckless and brash. Although the father and mother love both sons, the younger son is clearly their favorite. He seems bathed in a certain giftedness and charm that the parents and others find irresistible, even though he also seems to be headed toward a bad end.[2]

Because novels and films can go into more detail about a story than Jesus's short parables do, they can dwell on questions the parables do not address but that still may be relevant. Why, for example, does the father in the parable not intervene from the beginning and prevent his son from making such a terrible mistake? The father surely senses that nothing good will come from his son's actions, but he doesn't try to talk him out of it.

Jesus doesn't explore that issue, but Patrick K. Dooley, a scholar who has analyzed *A River Runs Through It* in light of the parable, sees a clue in the father's statement to the older son once the younger son comes home. In the parable, the father straightforwardly declares, "We had to celebrate and be glad, because this brother of yours was dead and is alive again; he was lost and is found" (Luke 15:32). The father doesn't try to justify or rationalize or explain the younger son's actions, or his own. The son is simply so loved that love can be the only response. In *A River Runs Through It*, everyone senses that Paul is rebellious, makes rash decisions, and is headed for trouble, but rather than "intervening, Paul's family is stymied by his verve and dash," Dooley says. The family realizes this younger son "is richly talented, charmingly likable and amply blessed—that is, that he has been divinely gifted and graced. Perhaps it is because his parents and older brother sense that Paul is a special person upon whom God's favor rests that their basic mode of dealing with him is a hands-off policy."[3]

Unconditional love drives both the novel and the parable. Both reveal what Dooley calls the "mystery of divine grace." God's chosen ones "are not perfect; indeed, they are often deeply flawed. . . . Accordingly, like the prodigal son before him, despite a dissolute and dangerous lifestyle, Paul is nonetheless graced and unconditionally loved."[4]

Dozens of other examples could be given to show the ways that the prodigal son parable has influenced literature and film. Eugene O'Neill draws on it in his one-act play, *The Rope*. Edward Arlington Robinson wrote a poem called "The Prodigal Son" in 1932. Franz Kafka gave the parable a significant twist in his short piece "Homecoming." Thomas Wolfe borrows some elements of the parable in his story "The Return of the Prodigal."

In film, critics have recognized influences of the parable in movies such as *Legends of the Fall*, which deals with troubled relationships between a father and sons, or *Iron Man*, in which Tony Stark inherits his inventor father's company and fortune but nearly loses everything—including his life—until he emerges in his new heroic identity. *The Godfather* films have prodigal son elements, and so does *A Knight's Tale*, when William returns to his father in a moving scene after a long separation during which he has become a knight.

The prodigal son parable also shows up repeatedly across the popular music spectrum. It has been treated in various ways in the songs of musical artists as diverse as Iron Maiden, Kid Rock, the Rolling Stones, Keith Green, Fred Hammond, and Casting Crowns. In 2016, Crowder released an album called *American Prodigal*. The inspiration for the title came from a sermon he heard from a pastor who focused on the literal meaning of the term "prodigal," which means "lavish." In a sense, we are all "prodigals" in that God has lavished this existence upon us. As Crowder told entertainment reporter Thomas Bruch, he felt that "if you've got your feet on the soil of the United

States of America, you've been lavished upon. It's a privilege to call this place home. We've been given a lot, now what should we do with it? What should we do with our inheritance?"[5]

Painters, novelists, poets, filmmakers, musicians, and other artists of all types draw inspiration from the prodigal son parable because Jesus's storytelling touched people where they live—parent-child relationships, sibling relationships, identity, personal freedom, consequences of sin, forgiveness, unconditional love, jealousy, salvation, second chances, and other themes. All that is packed into one short parable.

Why Does the Prodigal Son Story Strike So Deeply?

The mysterious power of the parable is what led Henri Nouwen to spend all those hours staring at Rembrandt's painting as he tried to probe why he felt so drawn to it. At first, he thought it was because he, like the prodigal son, felt lost and lonely, and longed to be welcomed home by the Father. That understanding satisfied him for a while, but later a friend suggested maybe he was really more like the older son in the story. Even though that had never occurred to Nouwen, it led him to relate to the story. He writes, "I suddenly saw myself in a completely new way. I saw my jealousy, my anger, my touchiness, doggedness and sullenness, and, most of all, my subtle self-righteousness. . . . For a time it became impossible to see how I could ever have thought of myself as the younger son. I was the elder son for sure."[6]

Even after that insight, Nouwen still wasn't finished being challenged by this parable. During a time of great inner pain, another friend led Nouwen to an insight that was just as jolting to him as when he realized he was like the elder son. She told him, "Whether you are the younger son or the elder son, you have to realize you are called to become the father."[7] In his work as pastor at L'Arche Daybreak, a community that ministers to people with intellectual disabilities, Nouwen's friend urged him to claim his true vocation and be a father who welcomes his children the way the father in the painting welcomes the prodigal son. Nouwen shifted his perspective on the painting and his own life in order to fully enter into this spiritual fatherhood.

Nouwen's very personal approach to this parable is not surprising. For many of us, the prodigal son story is hard to keep at a distance. We can't analyze it simply as an abstract theological statement. It works on us even deeper than we are consciously aware. My second novel, *A Son Comes Home*, is now considered a modern retelling of the prodigal son, but I didn't write it with that in mind. Even the title, which clearly points to the parable, was chosen by my publisher after I turned in the manuscript. I had titled the book something very different, but the publisher immediately saw the connection that I did not.

Years later, one of my colleagues was teaching the novel in an Introduction to Literature class and invited me to come and speak. Before she introduced me, she asked the class to make a list of anyone in the novel who could be considered a prodigal son, whether male or female. The list was long. By the end of the discussion of all the prodigals in the novel, I not only saw that issue as the major theme of the novel, but it actually started to feel overdone. If I had been consciously aware that the parable penetrated so many characters, scenes, plots, and subplots of the book, I might have toned it down a bit.

Throughout my life, I have clung to fragments of this parable for the hope it gives in its portrait of a heavenly Father who loves extravagantly. Fragments of the story, such as "he came to his senses" or "while he was still far off, his father ran to him" float through my head even when the story itself is not in front of me. The fact that these things are possible in the world is what I want to celebrate.

I can come to my senses.

I can repent.

I can turn toward home, and instead of having to explain myself, or grovel, or face the possibility of being ostracized, I can know that the Father is already running toward me.

That is my faith in a nutshell. I know of no other parable or any other story at all that captures salvation so vividly. I realize that my impression of the parable, like so many others I have described, emphasizes one aspect of it over others. I identify with the younger son, and I see in him my own desire for reconciliation with the heavenly Father.

From the Sports World to the Financial Arena, Prodigals Abound

The prodigal son may be the quintessential parable of reconciliation with the heavenly Father, but references to it also pop up in many other realms of life beyond the spiritual, from financial planning to sports to parenting advice. For example, focusing on the idea that the prodigal son asks for his inheritance early, one gift-planning consultant, Mike Strathdee, believes the story should serve as a "warning about giving children gifts before they are emotionally or spiritually mature enough to handle them properly." Would the story have turned out differently, the author wonders, "if the father knew what we now know about human brain development?" Although the story doesn't say how old the younger son is, the prefrontal cortex of the brain often isn't fully developed until the age of twenty-five, so people younger than that may not be able to fully understand the consequences of their actions. Strathdee quotes a financial expert who says that giving young people access to credit cards too early could be thought of as a form of child abuse.[8]

Strathdee's take certainly is not the usual treatment of the parable, but others have also taken the story in unexpected directions. Drawing on the prodigal son's squandering of resources, a governor in Nigeria accused his government of acting like that irresponsible son by securing a bond that would require many years of repayment and that might plunge the nation into economic misery.[9]

The sports world frequently makes use of prodigal son metaphors, such as when athletes return to former teams or redeem themselves from wayward behavior to find success. One of dozens of sports prodigals is former Super Bowl champion Sherman Williams. Now a motivational speaker and creator of a nonprofit organization that helps young people through athletics and other programs, Williams calls *himself* the prodigal son. His rise was rapid in the early 1990s as he went from being a high school football star to a college standout at the University of Alabama and, finally, during his rookie year with the Dallas Cowboys, a Super Bowl champion in 1995.[10]

Then, like the prodigal son, he chose a more rebellious path. He ended up in prison for conspiracy to distribute marijuana and passing counterfeit currency. When he emerged from that time in "the wilderness," as he calls it, he returned to the Father, determined to use his life for good. He says, "I wrote my book called *Crimson Cowboy* to give back to the community and to let my life be a testimony. By writing it, I'm able to put my story down on paper and the world can witness the miracle that God has worked in my life."[11] Profits from the book go to college scholarships and to his nonprofit organization to help others.

Most metaphorical uses of the prodigal son story focus on the younger, rebellious son, but occasionally the older son is highlighted. Political writer

Salim Furth, for example, refers to the older brother in an article about what he calls the "Forgotten Man." In this political sense, the Forgotten Man is the responsible, older-brotherish citizen who pays his taxes, does his job, stays out of trouble, keeps quiet, and helps the economy and society stay afloat. His grievance is that, while he does all the work, he ends up paying for the laziness or irresponsibility of the Prodigal Son citizen who refuses to behave appropriately. Government regulation and certain social programs and other government programs are a burden to the older brother and should be kept to a minimum, according to this perspective.[12]

While the Forgotten Man idea may be a way for those on certain parts of the political spectrum to see the older brother sympathetically, other metaphorical uses of that character from the parable take a more negative view. Fares Abou-Zakhim and his family had to flee their home in Syria in 2011 because of the bombing in the war that almost killed them. He lost his father in the fighting and also his house, job, cars, and money. Now living in Ohio, he lent his support to the fundraising efforts for Syrian refugees that his son's Catholic high school sponsored. In a prayer service for that effort, Bishop George V. Murry said that welcoming refugees shows the same kind of love the father of the parable showed in taking back his wayward son. Murry said, "We can either be like the father in this story, who welcomes his son back without a moment's hesitation, or we can be like the older son who was angry that the son, his brother, came back. Jesus asks of us to welcome those who are homeless, who are poor, who are the forgotten in our society."[13]

The prodigal son theme is so deeply entrenched in people's minds that it is sometimes applied even to inanimate objects. In Minnesota, a man named Cy Kubista started building a custom hot-rod car in 1960. It was a one-of-a-kind car, constructed over a period of years from scavenged parts and Kubista's creativity. As Matthew Stolle described it, "the car, in its various incarnations, would boast a 1925 Model-T body, a Lincoln automatic transmission, Edsel steering and transmission selection systems and front-end and rear-end assemblies, all of which Kubista designed and built himself."[14] Eventually, Kubista entered it in car shows and started winning. Magazines featured the car in their pages. Kubista took it to many road shows.

Kubista's love for the car eventually collided with his love for his wife and three children, who needed some of the time and resources he was devoting to the machine. Reluctantly, he sold it. Later, he bought it back. Eventually, he sold it again. Then in 2017, fifty-seven years after he first started working on the car, Kubista got it back. His son bought it for his now eighty-four-year-old father. Kubista was overjoyed. As Stolle puts it, for "the man who had built the hot rod from scratch and who hadn't seen his creation in years, it was like the return of the prodigal son." Kubista tearfully told his wife, "It's home. She's home."[15]

Why Did Jesus Tell This Parable?

People feel connected to the prodigal son theme for a multitude of reasons, but what was the message Jesus intended? Why did he tell this parable? The prodigal son parable and the two that precede it were prompted by a complaint by the Pharisees and teachers of the law, who noticed that "tax collectors and sinners were all gathering around to hear Jesus." Their complaint was that "this man welcomes sinners and eats with them" (Luke 15:1). They meant it as a derogatory accusation, but Jesus embraced the charge. He came to announce and launch the kingdom of God, and he intended to find the lost—the sinners, the unwanted, the despised, the lowly—and save them and invite them into that kingdom.

Rather than answer the accusation directly, he told three parables. The first is about a lost sheep. If you have a hundred sheep but one gets lost, don't you put all your effort into finding and restoring the lost one? Jesus says, "I tell you that in the same way there will be more rejoicing in heaven over one sinner who repents than over ninety-nine righteous persons who do not need to repent" (v. 7).

He followed that with a parable about a lost coin. If a woman has ten valuable coins and loses one, doesn't she search everywhere until she finds it, and then rejoice over it with friends and neighbors?

Finally, Jesus raised the stakes by telling a parable in which what is "lost" are human beings rather than an animal or an object. Although we now most commonly call this the parable of the prodigal son, it is actually the story of two lost sons, one younger and one older. Both are lost in their own ways. The younger son finds forgiveness. The fate of the older son is left untold.

"Prodigal son" is not an accurate name for the parable, not only because it concerns two sons rather than one, but also because "prodigal" is a misleading word to describe the younger man. "Prodigal" means spending or giving in a lavish or extravagant way. Because the term is so often associated with this parable, many people mistakenly believe the word means "wayward" or "rebellious." The younger son is "prodigal" in one sense—when he spends recklessly after receiving his inheritance. But some commentators—such as Timothy Keller, who titled his book on this parable *Prodigal God*—believe the term is a better fit for the father in the story, who loves his sons extravagantly.

If Jesus told the parables of the lost sheep, lost coin, and lost sons as a response to the Pharisees' complaint that he was eating with sinners, then who in the parable corresponds to those critics? Keller says that the tax collectors and sinners correspond to the younger son, and Jesus's critics are represented by the older brother. He points out that the Pharisees and teachers of the law "held to the traditional morality of their upbringing. They studied and obeyed the Scripture. They worshiped faithfully and prayed constantly."[16] Still, they were lost. That doesn't mean the tax collectors and sinners were any better off. They were lost too. Keller writes that each of these "life-paths are dead ends, and that every thought the human race has had about how to connect to God has been wrong." Jesus told the parable not to comfort but to "shatter our categories."[17]

Fleeing to a Distant Country

Asking for an inheritance early may sound a little odd to people in our day, but to the original listeners, it would have sounded absolutely shocking. Martin Saunders says that "in a modern context we miss the total outrageousness of the son's request. Since such a transaction would only ever take place when a father was about to die and could no longer head the family or its business, the son is effectively saying to his father 'I wish you were dead.'"[18]

The father could have flatly refused this request, but he chooses not to forcibly prevent his son from rebelling. The young man follows this outrage by quickly going to a "distant country" and squandering his inheritance in wild living. Spiritually speaking, what is this distant country? What is it to wish the father dead? Many people *do* wish the heavenly Father dead, or believe that he already *is* dead, or that he does not exist and never did. They travel from early belief in him to the distant country where they no longer believe he is alive, or if he is, where he is no longer relevant to them.

In that country they can look around and say, "What Father? He isn't here." They can live their lives without bothering with him. Living in the distant country may also mean succumbing, as the young son does, to various forms of "wild living"—self-destructive behavior, squandered opportunities, a wasted life. The young man in the parable eventually comes to his senses in that country and returns to the father, but spiritually, many choose never to return. Nouwen describes "home" as the knowledge that you are beloved by the Father, so fleeing home for the distant country "is a denial of the spiritual reality that I belong to God with every part of my being, that God holds me safe in an eternal embrace, that I am indeed carved in the palms of God's hands and hidden in their shadows."[19]

The key to avoiding the seductive lure of the "distant country" is learning to accept—to really know deep inside ourselves—the unconditional love of God; to know that we don't need to earn his love or prove ourselves to him; to know that anything else we try as a *replacement* of him—the new place, the new thrill, the new pleasure, the new person—is chasing after the wind. The son never intended to end up starving among the pigs. No doubt when he first set out, his rebellion felt like freedom and control. Spiritually speaking, living among the pigs does not always manifest itself in the economic calamity the son faces. You can be financially comfortable or even be a billionaire and still wallow in that desperate pigpen of cynicism, anger, recrimination, greed, malice, and self-absorption.

The son wakes up to his plight, but that awareness comes at a high price. He is dehumanized, poor, alone, hungry, and devoid of any plan for the future. However, hitting the bottom also makes him less entitled, less self-sufficient, less arrogant, less disrespectful of his father and family. Starting from this low point, he can decide to launch himself back toward love and sanity. He has reached the end of his own physical, psychological, and spiritual resources, but he realizes he doesn't have to stay there or die there. He can reach toward love.

Hitting rock bottom isn't always necessary for people to come to their senses, but a change of outlook on their reality does have to happen. Those who turn to the Father have to conclude that, first, they no longer want to live in the spiritually impoverished, distant country in which they are now living, and, second, returning to the Father is the answer. Waking up to his plight did not in itself guarantee that the son would return to his father. He could have looked for some other way out of his predicament—violence, self-destruction, resignation. It took courage for him to decide to humble himself and return, especially since he didn't know what his reception would be. Repentance does not come easily, but you can't reach the Father without it.

Even when he decides to return, the son still tries to retain some control of the situation. He rehearses a speech that he never gets the chance to fully deliver. Feeling his unworthiness, he wants to repent, but he also wants to make a deal. He is willing to be treated like a hired servant. The father doesn't give him a chance to negotiate any deals, though. Nor does he even wait for the son to make it all the way home. While the young man is "still a long way off," the father runs to him—an act out of keeping with the dignity of fathers of that era—and embraces him. He calls for his son to be lavished with new clothes, a ring, and a feast. It's a happy ending for the younger son, but for another family member, it's an outrage.

The Older Son

When I first started reading the prodigal son parable, I was aware of the older brother in the story, but he always seemed like a tacked-on element at the end rather than a central figure. The real ending for me was the younger son's reconciliation with the father. Jesus could have left out the grouchy older brother, and that would have been fine with me. If I gave that older brother any thought at all, I had to admit that he did seem to have a legitimate grievance. Why did his younger brother get to just waltz back into the family and have everything handed to him? But that's part of the beauty of forgiveness, right? That you get a second chance? That you are restored to relationship with the Father, even though you don't deserve it?

It never occurred to me that the older son represents the audience to whom Jesus is telling the parable—the Pharisees and teachers of the law. They were "good," but self-righteous and self-sufficient. Unfortunately, their goodness (adherence to the law) does not include generosity toward others whom the Father chooses to save. They are lost in ways that are hard for them to recognize.

One of the tragedies of the older son is his lack of belief in his father's abundance—of material things, of love, of attention. "You are always with me, and everything I have is yours," the father says in verse 31. The older son will be taken care of. He is loved. He will have plenty. But will he ruin it for himself out of resentment that his brother gets something he doesn't deserve? It's an ugly impulse, but one that is easy for "good" people to fall into. Jesus saw it in the Pharisees, but today he might see it in many long-term Christians. It's an us-versus-them mentality, a mindset that sees those who are not Christians not as lost brothers and sisters to be welcomed in but as the enemy to be defeated. You can see this attitude played out on social media. Staunch Christians treat those who are not "in" as people to be dismissed, or railed against, or hated, or stereotyped, or mocked—anything but loved. If pressed, we might *say* we love those outsiders, but . . . and there would always be the "but," which would lead us back into the enemy talk. Jesus is teaching that this is lostness. It's a different kind of lostness than the younger son practices, but it is lostness just the same.

There are more parallels between the two sons than may at first be apparent. Both sons come home—the younger from the distant country and the older from the field. Both rebel against their father. The younger son does it in a more obvious way, but the older son refuses to come inside to the party and then angrily rebukes the father when the man comes outside to plead with his son. Both are offered a second chance by a loving father. The younger son takes it. The fate of the older son is left unknown. The party he is boycotting could include him if he wanted it to, and he could take part in the joy of forgiveness if he could soften his heart toward his brother and accept his father's love for both of them. Will he do it?

By the time the older son comes home from the field, the party for his younger brother is already in full swing. The father doesn't consult the older brother about it. He doesn't need to. "But we had to celebrate and be glad," the father tells him, "because this brother of yours was dead and is alive again; he was lost and is found" (v. 32).

There are many ways to fall into the trap of being like the older brother. Self-sufficiency is one of them—the idea that *I'm good enough as I am and don't need Jesus to save me.* Or maybe it's summed up in the idea that *I may not be so great, but at least I'm better than all these other people.*

No one is *entitled* to God's love and forgiveness. You can't earn it. He offers it only out of his own mercy, not your own worthiness. No matter which character in the parable you relate to most, God the Father has started a party to which everyone is invited. The younger brother has already accepted the invitation and is inside celebrating. He is there not because he deserves to be but because God loves him that much. If you are an older-brother type, he has invited you too. Perhaps you're still standing there deciding whether you should go in. Will pride or arrogance stop you? Are you too annoyed by how other believers sometimes behave to want to have anything to do with them?

Are you holding out for the Father to arrange everything on your own terms? Maybe it's time to come inside and enjoy the celebration.

Notes

1. Henri J. M. Nouwen, *The Return of the Prodigal Son: A Story of Homecoming* (New York: Doubleday, 1992), 15.

2. Robert Redford, Craig Sheffer, Brad Pitt, Tom Skerritt, Brenda Blethyn, Emily Lloyd, Mark Isham, Philippe Rousselot, and Norman Maclean, *A River Runs Through It*, dir. by Robert Redford (Culver City, CA: Columbia Pictures, 1992).

3. Patrick Dooley, "The Prodigal Son Parable And Maclean's A River Runs Through It," *Renascence* 58, no. 2 (Winter 2005), 164–76.

4. Dooley, "The Prodigal Son Parable," 169.

5. Thomas Bruch, "'Folktronica' musician Crowder headlines the Winter Jam tour this weekend," *Peoria JournalStar*, February 8, 2017, https://www.pjstar.com/entertainmentlife /20170208/folktronica-musician-crowder-headlines-winter-jam-tour-this-weekend.

6. Nouwen, *Return of the Prodigal Son*, 20.

7. Nouwen, *Return of the Prodigal Son*, 22.

8. Mike Strathdee, "Preventing Prodigals," *ChristianWeek*, January 26, 2017, http://www .christianweek.org/preventing-prodigals/.

9. "1bn Eurobond: Fayose knocks FG, says APC govt is behaving like prodigal son," *Vanguard*, February 10, 2017, https://www.vanguardngr.com/2017/02/1bn-eurobond-fayose -knocks-fg-says-apc-govt-behaving-like-prodigal-son/.

10. Heather Osbourne, "NFL Champion Sherman Williams to Visit NWF State," *The Destin Log*, February 16, 2017, https://www.thedestinlog.com/news/20170216/nfl-champion -sherman-williams-to-visit-nwf-state.

11. Osbourne, "Sherman Williams to Visit NWF State."

12. Salim Furth, "Who is the 'Forgotten Man'? A Historical Look," *The Daily Signal*, February 14, 2017, https://www.dailysignal.com/2017/02/14/who-is-the-forgotten-man-a -historical-look/.

13. Charita Goshay, "Local Students Raise Awareness, Funds for Syrian Refugees," *The Canton Repository*, February 15, 2017, https://www.cantonrep.com/news/20170215/local-students -raise-awareness-funds-for-syrian-refugees.

14. Matthew Stolle, "Award-winning Hot Rod Returns to Family," *PostBulletin*, February 8, 2017, https://www.postbulletin.com/news/local/award-winning-hot-rod-returns-to-family /article_43fa8ac4-9d76-52bf-9c49-0ab5cb2ff66b.html.

15. Stolle, "Hot Rod Returns."

16. Timothy Keller, *The Prodigal God: Recovering the Heart of the Christian Faith* (New York: Dutton, 2008), 8.

17. Keller, *Prodigal God*, 10, 11.

18. Martin Saunders, "Six Amazing Things You Might Not Know about the Prodigal Son," *Christian Today*, December 10, 2016, https://www.christiantoday.com/article/six-amazing -things-you-might-not-know-about-the-prodigal-son/102788.htm.

19. Nouwen, *Return of the Prodigal Son*, 37.

Digging Deeper

1. When you think of the prodigal son parable, with which character do you most naturally identify? Why?

2. This chapter explores the idea that, in some senses, we might have opportunity or occasion to be *all* the characters in the parable. Do you see ways in which all three major characters might connect to you?

3. If you had to encapsulate the meaning of the prodigal son parable in one sentence, what would it be?

4. This chapter discusses works of literature, film, and art that employ the prodigal son theme. Can you think of other examples? Why do authors, artists, and musicians so often turn to this theme?

5. For you, what is the most powerful moment in the parable? Describe why you find that part of the story so moving or significant.

Go to https://www.thefoundrypublishing.com/12NT/LeaderGuide for a free downloadable leader's guide that includes more questions for reflection as well as activities for use in a small group setting.

3

The Good Samaritan // Charles Herbert Moore // c. 1840-1930

The Good Samaritan

[25] *On one occasion an expert in the law stood up to test Jesus. "Teacher," he asked, "what must I do to inherit eternal life?"*

[26] *"What is written in the Law?" he replied. "How do you read it?"*

[27] *He answered, "'Love the Lord your God with all your heart and with all your soul and with all your strength and with all your mind'; and, 'Love your neighbor as yourself.'"*

[28] *"You have answered correctly," Jesus replied. "Do this and you will live."*

[29] *But he wanted to justify himself, so he asked Jesus, "And who is my neighbor?"*

[30] *In reply Jesus said: "A man was going down from Jerusalem to Jericho, when he was attacked by robbers. They stripped him of his clothes, beat him and went away, leaving him half dead.* [31] *A priest happened to be going down the same road, and when he saw the man, he passed by on the other side.* [32] *So too, a Levite, when he came to the place and saw him, passed by on the other side.* [33] *But a Samaritan, as he traveled, came where the man was; and when he saw him, he took pity on him.* [34] *He went to him and bandaged his wounds, pouring on oil and wine. Then he put the man on his own donkey, brought him to an inn and took care of him.* [35] *The next day he took out two denarii and gave them to the innkeeper. 'Look after him,' he said, 'and when I return, I will reimburse you for any extra expense you may have.'*

[36] *"Which of these three do you think was a neighbor to the man who fell into the hands of robbers?"*

[37] *The expert in the law replied, "The one who had mercy on him."*

Jesus told him, "Go and do likewise."

—Luke 10:25–37

I HAVE TO ADMIT that the Good Samaritan story has never been one of my favorites. I cringe when I see that I'll be in a church service where a pastor is going to preach about it. The reason I shy away from the story is that I find it to be one of the most guilt-inducing parables in the Bible. I try to be a reasonably compassionate person, giving money to missions and ministries for the poor and helping out in whatever ways I can, but how could I possibly live up to this man's example? Like the prodigal son, the Good Samaritan is a two-thousand-year-old fictional character who has transcended the original story in which he appeared and has become well known even to people who have never opened a Bible. Just as Jesus never used the term "prodigal son" when he told that parable, he also never used the term "Good Samaritan" to describe the main character of the parable now known by that name.

Call someone a Good Samaritan, and people know exactly what you mean. You're describing a compassionate person, often one who displays unusual courage or generosity to help others. The Good Samaritan won't ask for credit or repayment, and the person who is helped doesn't have to do or be anyone special in order to receive the kindness.

The Good Samaritan is such a positive character that many people want their businesses and ministries to be named after him. Across the world, people have named hospitals, ministry organizations, homeless missions, clinics, churches, and educational institutions Good Samaritan in order to associate themselves with this selfless man. Many states have Good Samaritan laws to protect citizens who act compassionately in tragic circumstances. Artists have depicted this character, and songs have celebrated him.

Those who have appropriated the label "Good Samaritan" have also redefined it. Who is this Good Samaritan Jesus described? Is he merely a nice guy, or is there a deeper significance not always captured by popular depictions of him? What is the significance of identifying him as a Samaritan? How closely does Jesus expect us to follow his example?

First Comes the Lawyer, with a Test

As with many other parables, Jesus told the parable of the Good Samaritan in order to answer a specific question. The parable is actually the answer to a *follow-up* question, indicating that if the lawyer who was questioning Jesus hadn't persisted, Jesus might never have told the story at all. Who is asking these questions? I call him a lawyer, which is how many Bible translations and commentators refer to him. Others translate the word with such varied phrases as teacher of the law, theologian, expert in Mosaic Law, or religious scholar. Other than this title, we don't know anything about this man. He was a scriptural expert, and he "stood up to test Jesus." That sounds aggressive, and maybe it was, since the Gospels are full of people trying to trap Jesus with tricky, insincere questions designed to embarrass or discredit him.

On the other hand, it's possible that his motivation was not so sinister. After all, being an expert in the law was his job, and Jesus had emerged as a prominent teacher about whom big claims were being made. Shouldn't the Scripture expert question him in order to test his teaching? In any case, the question he asked was not unreasonable: "Teacher, what must I do to inherit eternal life?"

Not surprisingly, given Jesus's usual methods of handling people who were testing him, he did not answer the question directly. Instead, he answered the question with questions. "What is written in the Law? How do you read it?"

Jesus asked not only for the words of the law but also for this Scripture expert's interpretation of it. Whatever the lawyer's motivations, Jesus answered him respectfully, giving a nod to his expertise. The lawyer gave a solid answer. The first verse he cited comes from Deuteronomy 6:4–5, part of the *Shema*—one of the most familiar portions of Scripture to Jews—about loving the Lord with all your heart, soul, strength, and mind. The second verse comes from Leviticus 19:18, giving the command to love your neighbor as yourself. Jesus told him he had answered correctly. Do that, and he would live. Good job. The expert passed the test. That might have signaled the end of the encounter. Question asked and answered. Go do it. End of story. If I had been questioning Jesus, I might have thanked him and walked away.

Our lawyer, however, was not satisfied. He passed the test, but he might have started to wonder, why was *he* being tested? Wasn't he supposed to be the one testing Jesus? So instead of leaving it there, he raised the stakes by asking another question. The verse says he "wanted to justify himself." In what sense? Since Jesus had turned things around and had become the interrogator rather than the interrogated, did the lawyer want to get back in the game and take control again? Or was the justification he sought more about his own behavior regarding the scriptures he had just cited? It's fine to cite these well-known verses and then be told to do them, but how far did they extend? Had the lawyer done enough to satisfy them? How narrowly could he define neighbor and still be thought to have fulfilled the law?

As commentator Craig A. Evans puts it, "The legal expert, by his qualifying question, may have been trying to find a loophole."[1] If that's the kind of self-justifying, loophole-finding move the lawyer is making, then I have to confess that I too am sometimes guilty of it. I want to do the right thing—I want to love my neighbor, but what are the limits? What is the cost? Jesus answered with a story that has made generations of Christians squirm.

Defining the Neighbor

"Who is my neighbor?" asked the lawyer. This time Jesus did not answer the question with a question, but neither did he answer the question directly. Instead, he told a story (and *then* asked a question). The parable that has had such an enormous impact on the world is short, taking up only six verses of the Bible.

A man going down from Jerusalem to Jericho is attacked by robbers, stripped, and left for dead. This was a realistic scenario on that road in Jesus's day. His audience could easily picture the scene. But even though the victim is half dead, there is still hope for him if help arrives in time. Suspense builds in this very short story. Who will save him? Along comes the priest. Thank God! A rescuer has arrived. But the priest passes by on the other side. Not his problem. Disappointing, but still, all is not lost. Maybe someone else will be more willing to help. Next comes the Levite. Will the story now have a happy ending? He too passes by on the other side. Will the man be left to die?

Why did the priest and the Levite not help? This is a story of *action* (and inaction) rather than dialogue or explanation, so the *why* of their behavior is left unanswered. Some commentators have assumed their reason for not helping might be their fear of violating purity laws, but many other scholars dismiss that as an excuse. Amy-Jill Levine, for example, writes that, "To follow the Torah, the priest should have checked to see if the man was alive and, finding him alive, should have helped him. Should he have discovered a corpse, he should have covered it and then immediately gone for help."[2] Even if the priest had been concerned about purity violations because of how encountering a possible corpse might interfere with his temple duties, the story points out that he was going "down" *from* Jerusalem—away from it—not up *to* Jerusalem, toward those priestly rituals.[3]

However, even if Levine is right, and there was technically no purity barrier keeping them from helping the half-dead man, that doesn't mean they might not have used those purity rules as an excuse for inaction. If they spent so much of their lives avoiding situations that made them ritually unclean, was it easier simply to objectify the man as a possible rule violation than to see him as a fellow human being in need? Does their religiosity get in the way of their compassion? Is this story somehow an indictment of the religious elite who saw themselves as too superior to help someone in need? Once again, Levine says no: "There is nothing that makes a priest and even less a Levite part of the 'elite.' Priests and Levites may have had neither wealth nor status."[4]

Everything about the story, then, resists the idea that the people avoiding the injured man are anything different from what we in the audience are—ordinary people trying to make our way through life. Their unstated reasons for action could be any of the ones we use—fear, busyness, reluctance to take on burdens that are not our responsibility, a belief that someone else will help, a prejudice that maybe the person is not deserving of our help. So why are they identified as a priest and Levite at all?

Levine says Jesus is using the "rule of three" that is common in many stories, such as "Goldilocks and the Three Bears" or "The Three Little Pigs," or many others. She writes, "For Jesus's audience, and for any synagogue congregation today, the third of the group is obvious. Mention a priest and a Levite, and anyone who knows anything about Judaism will know that the third person is an Israelite."[5] Jesus, however, springs a surprise. The third person is not the expected Israelite who will sweep in and do the right thing. The third person is someone the audience would not expect to be in this story at all—a Samaritan, an enemy, someone who should never be given the role of hero in a story. Jesus's parable is a story about breaking down barriers that separate people, and the entrance of this despised—but good!—Samaritan into the story is the first startling example.

Remember the question Jesus is answering: who is my neighbor? This question implicitly also asks, who is *not* my neighbor? In other words, whom can I safely ignore, or from whom may I safely withhold the love that Scripture demands? Commentator Simon J. Kistemaker explains that the Jewish audience listening to the parable lived in a "circular world" with themselves at the center, then immediate family in the next ring, then kinspeople, then Jews in general: "The word *neighbor* has a reciprocal meaning: he is a brother to me and I to him. Thus the circle is one of self-interest and ethnocentrism. The lines were carefully drawn to ensure the well-being of those who were inside and to deny help to those who were outside."[6]

The Samaritan in the parable immediately sets about demolishing those carefully drawn lines, first by appearing as the unexpected hero of the story and then by his specific actions. Unlike the lawyer who is questioning Jesus, the Samaritan does not ask any questions before he offers help. He does not ask, *Who is the victim? Is he someone of my ethnicity or faith or background? Is he deserving of my aid? Am I obligated to help him? Will I be repaid if I help him? Will my trip be thrown helplessly off schedule if I help? Am I inviting unnecessary complications into my life by bothering with this man?* The Samaritan sweeps aside any barriers that might prevent him from helping and acts by taking the man to the innkeeper and paying the expenses for his recuperation until the Samaritan can return. He acts swiftly and lovingly and asks for nothing in return.

One question that arises with any parable is, with whom are we as readers supposed to identify? Who are we in the story? The victim? The priest? The Levite? The Good Samaritan? The innkeeper? Part of the power of the parable is that most of us can identify with every character in it in different ways. I have been the priest and Levite crossing the road when I see the person who needs me—either because I don't care enough, or I'm busy, or I'm afraid, or I harbor unacknowledged prejudices that make me believe I should keep the needy person at a distance because of his or her differences from me in some aspect of identity such as ethnicity or ideology or religion or race.

I can relate to the innkeeper, faithfully carrying out my duty when the situation calls for it—and when I get something for myself in return—and when it comfortably fits into the calling or routine I believe is my own.

I can identify with the crime victim, knocked into helplessness by tragedy I do not deserve. Who will rescue me? Who will act toward me with love beyond what I deserve or could ever repay? What if it is my enemy—or someone I have perceived as an enemy—who answers that call? Can I be vulnerable enough to accept help from that person whom, in other circumstances, I might have scorned? Am I willing to redefine someone based on their loving response to me in the time of my deepest need?

In my best moments I can identify with the Good Samaritan. I decide—at whatever cost—to follow that impulse deep within to *act* in love. Instead of fleeing the person who makes me cringe, I push myself toward that person and make their problems my own. I follow through until I see the situation set right. I willingly pay the price.

One reason the Good Samaritan parable has always prompted guilt for me is that the Samaritan himself seems to set such a high, perhaps impossible, standard for what it means to be a neighbor. But is that the story's intent? I have often thought of the Good Samaritan as giving everything—including a blank check—to rescue the stranger. I want to give, I want to be a neighbor, but does that mean there are *no* limits? What about responsibilities I already have in my life—partnering with my wife to raise our children, showing up and doing my work as a professor and writer, serving in my church, paying bills, handling crises, and keeping the many commitments to others that I have already made? Can I do all that and still be a good neighbor, or are those things to be considered selfish and expendable and to be dropped at the first sign of need from elsewhere? Are there no limits?

In one sense the parable *is* about abolishing limits. The person I should consider as my neighbor is not limited to someone who is like me or in my family or ethnic group or religion or race. Those limits do not apply. On the other hand, the Samaritan does set limits. He pays for the care of the man—very generous!—but he goes on his way rather than doing that care himself. His impulse is toward giving, but he is creative about it. His trip is *delayed* because he helps the man, but he does not *cancel* his trip. Perhaps he is thinking something along the lines of, "The money to care for that man has to come from somewhere. I had better not miss this business trip."

The Samaritan acts compassionately, but he is not expected to fix *everything* in order to be a neighbor. He doesn't chase down the robbers and bring them to justice. He doesn't create a police force to patrol that dangerous road. He doesn't take responsibility for *every* victim of crime in that area. He doesn't assume responsibility for the victim for the rest of his life. There are limits to his time and resources and capabilities, but he is considered the Good Samaritan—the true neighbor—because his impulse is love. He *acts* rather than makes excuses. He does not let limitation, fear, or prejudice paralyze him into inaction as the priest and Levite do. He does what is in his power.

That way of looking at the parable is liberating to me because the message is, do what you can. Don't let the fact that you can't do everything prevent you from doing something. The parable should not paralyze us; rather, it should set us in motion. Show mercy. To a neighbor. Someone nearby. Without calculation. Without fretting too much about how it will throw off your schedule, how worthy the person is, or how it will solve some problem the person embodies. You see a need. You do something. Someone is better off. You move on.

Latching onto the Samaritan's Good Name

The six verses of the Bible that embody the Good Samaritan's story have led hundreds of organizations to associate themselves in name with this good man. Some of them connect to the parable in a general way, standing for a compassionate purpose such as healthcare or housing for the elderly. Other organizations connect to a more specific element of the story, such as the idea that everyone is deserving of help, regardless of which racial, ethnic, religious, or other category into which the person might fall. The mission statement of The Good Samaritan Home in Evansville, Indiana, says, "In keeping with the image offered by our name, The Good Samaritan Home is committed to extending God's love to neighbors who need our help along the road of life, and to do that with respect for the sanctity of life."[7] The Good Samaritan Church in Whittier, California, says that its mission is "to minister healing to all who have been left broken, wounded, or bruised by the side of life's busy road."[8]

Good Samaritan Ministries is an organization that runs programs to find housing for the homeless, sponsors initiatives to help low-income individuals and families reach their financial goals, and helps churches reach out to needy people in various ways. They believe their "job as good neighbors is to be there for one another and to work together to affirm the dignity entitled to every person as a child of God. We are inclusive, we are collaborative, and we bring our neighbors—individuals, businesses, local governments, faith-based organizations, other nonprofits—together to follow the example of the Good Samaritan and heed Jesus's words: 'Go and do likewise.'"[9]

One of the largest and most influential ministries that connects its mission specifically to the Good Samaritan story is Samaritan's Purse, which provides crisis and disaster relief, refugee help, water and construction projects, medical missions, and other services around the world. It also conducts Operation Christmas Child, in which churches and other groups fill shoeboxes with toys and other supplies for Christmas gifts for children around the world. The organization's website says that the parable "of the Good Samaritan gives a clear picture of God's desire for us to help those in desperate need wherever we find them. . . . For over 40 years, Samaritan's Purse has done our utmost to follow Christ's command by going to the aid of the world's poor, sick, and suffering."[10]

Hundreds of other examples could be listed. Of course, naming something "Good Samaritan" doesn't mean that the organization automatically embraces everything the biblical story stands for. A name only carries you so far. But the ideals around which an organization is founded do matter, and as it carries out its mission over the years, that influence of this good man as a role model may continue to affect how the institution as a whole and the individuals within it approach their work. The world is a better place because Jesus told his six-verse fictional story about a man who refused to walk away from someone in need.

Law

Jesus's imaginary compassionate Samaritan has even had an impact on secular laws. Like the priest and Levite who cross to the other side of the road to avoid helping the man in need, some people today are also reluctant to help someone in need in an emergency situation. In a litigious society, the fear of being blamed if something goes wrong keeps people on the sidelines. In a messy, dangerous situation, no one wants to risk getting sued if they help in a way that doesn't work or that inadvertently leads to more harm. Good Samaritan laws have been passed to encourage citizens to behave more like the Samaritan than the priest or Levite. These laws are intended to protect from litigation average citizens—anyone who isn't a medical professional—who step in to help when they witness an accident or someone in need.

In San Antonio, Texas, in 2014, a woman saw a one-year-old boy sitting alone in a locked car on a hot day. He did not look distressed, but the woman didn't want to take any chances. She wanted to break into the car to rescue him, but a security guard warned her to wait and told her she could be arrested if she broke the window. Instead, she decided, "I don't care if I get arrested; I'm going to save this baby."[11] She smashed the windshield with a tire iron and crawled through to get the child.

Because of the Good Samaritan law in Texas, the woman was not arrested or charged. Clearly, her only intent was to help a child in a dangerous situation, and the law is set up to honor and protect that kind of behavior. The security guard might have been willing, like the priest and the Levite, to stand by and do nothing as the minutes ticked away, but the woman had the courage to set aside her own comfort and act. An investigation using surveillance footage revealed that the father had left the child in the car for about forty minutes. He said he forgot the child was in there and was charged with child endangerment.[12]

What if a church or other organization wants to feed homeless people by giving them food that people have donated from grocery stores? Would those groups be liable for the quality of the donated food? Could they be sued or criminally prosecuted if someone got sick from it? Should they follow the example of the priest and Levite and avoid helping in this way? Once again, the legal system has learned from the biblical Good Samaritan, and laws have been passed to protect those who want to help needy people by donating food. At the U.S. federal level, the Bill Emerson Good Samaritan Food Donation Act makes it possible for donors and feeding programs to operate without fear of prosecution or liability that might arise from the quality of the food donated as long as they are not grossly negligent. Because this law takes away much of the fear of helping others, countless people are fed, and good food does not go to waste.[13]

To answer a lawyer's question, Jesus told a very short story about a Samaritan man, to whom later generations have attached the word "good." That character has captured the idealism of countless individuals and organizations who want to do one thing: help people. Because the Samaritan is so selfless, he can be a daunting example to try to imitate. But Jesus was not setting a standard that only the most exalted saints could reach.

How do I know if I'm living like the Good Samaritan? The details will look different from person to person, but here are some questions I ask myself: Is my life characterized by tearing down barriers that separate me from others—barriers of race, wealth, ethnicity, or religious background? Is my life characterized by a spirit of generosity and selfless action rather than clinging desperately to everything that I consider "mine"? Do I approach my life as an opportunity to give and connect to others, or do I treat others as merely a means to improve or protect my own status? How do I treat the most vulnerable—the homeless, the poor, the immigrant, the ex-convict, the "undeserving"? Jesus finished his discussion with the lawyer not by calling for more philosophizing or agonizing or hairsplitting over who counts as a neighbor. Instead, he concluded with a simple statement that is still relevant for us today: "Go and do likewise."

Notes

1. Craig A. Evans, *Luke*, New International Biblical Commentary (Peabody, MA: Hendrickson, 2008), 176.

2. Amy-Jill Levine, *Short Stories by Jesus: The Enigmatic Parables of a Controversial Rabbi* (New York: HarperCollins, 2014), 92.

3. Levine, *Short Stories*, 93.

4. Levine, *Short Stories,* 90.

5. Levine, *Short Stories*, 95.

6. Simon J. Kistemaker, *The Parables: Understanding the Stories Jesus Told* (Grand Rapids: Baker Books, 2002), 141.

7. "Welcome to Good Samaritan Home," Good Samaritan Home, n.d., https://goodsam home.org/.

8. "Our Mission Statement," Good Samaritan Church, Whittier, CA, n.d., http://whittiermcc.org/.

9. "Who Is My Neighbor?" Good Samaritan Ministries, n.d., https://www.goodsamminis tries.com/who-we-are/who-is-my-neighbor/.

10. "About Us," Samaritan's Purse, n.d., https://www.samaritanspurse.org/our-ministry/about-us/.

11. Martha Neil, "Citing Good Samaritan Law, Police Don't Charge Woman Who Broke into Hot Car to Save Baby," *ABA Journal*, September 22, 2014, http://www.abajournal.com/news/article/police_cite_good_samaritan_law_dont_charge_woman_who_broke_into_hot_car_to/.

12. Neil, "Police Don't Charge Woman."

13. "The Federal Bill Emerson Good Samaritan Food Donation Act," Feeding America, n.d., https://www.feedingamerica.org/about-us/partners/become-a-product-partner/food-partners.

Digging Deeper

1. Early in this chapter, the author says that he sometimes shies away from the Good Samaritan parable because it can come across as "one of the most guilt-inducing parables in the Bible." Do you see it that way? Do you think that was Jesus's intent when he told it? What would you suggest as the best response to this parable?

2. Think of ways in which you can identify with the various characters in this parable. As the chapter discusses, have you sometimes played the part of the priest and Levite? The beaten-up victim? The innkeeper? The Good Samaritan? What can you learn from each of these characters?

3. When hospitals and other organizations adopt the Good Samaritan name, what traits of that character do these institutions desire to embody?

4. Jesus tells this parable to answer the question "Who is my neighbor?" Given the social and political realities of our day, in what ways do we also have to confront that question? How can Jesus's parable guide us?

Go to https://www.thefoundrypublishing.com/12NT/LeaderGuide for a free downloadable leader's guide that includes more questions for reflection as well as activities for use in a small group setting.

Jesus's Big Ideas

4

The Parable of the Mote and the Beam // Domenico Fetti // c. 1620

Judge Not

¹ "Do not judge, or you too will be judged. ² For in the same way you judge others, you will be judged, and with the measure you use, it will be measured to you.

³ "Why do you look at the speck of sawdust in your brother's eye and pay no attention to the plank in your own eye? ⁴ How can you say to your brother, 'Let me take the speck out of your eye,' when all the time there is a plank in your own eye? ⁵ You hypocrite, first take the plank out of your own eye, and then you will see clearly to remove the speck from your brother's eye."

—Matthew 7:1-5

"DON'T JUDGE ME." How many times have you heard someone say it? Maybe you have even said it yourself. I've heard it hundreds of times, sometimes lightheartedly, sometimes seriously. If someone cuts a too-generous piece of dessert, they might jokingly say, "Don't judge me. I'm really hungry today." A teenager trying to explain to her parents why she chose a particular boyfriend, of whom she knows her parents will not approve, might say, "Stop judging him," or, "Quit judging us," or "Don't judge me for choosing him."

No one likes to be judged, and no one likes to be accused of being judgmental. When people *are* judgmental, they rarely call it that. They might instead refer to their judgments as "standing up for what's right," or "common sense," or "discernment."

While most of the Scripture passages in this book are more likely to be recited by Christians than by nonbelievers, "judge not" is one that nonbelievers are just as likely to know and recite, often as an indictment of Christians. The perception of Christians as judgmental is as strong today as ever and has kept countless people from becoming followers of Jesus Christ. When Jesus spoke against being judgmental, he zeroed in on a problem that would be just as relevant to readers two thousand years later as on the day he said it.

In 2007 David Kinnaman and Gabe Lyons published a book called *unChristian*, which was based on thousands of interviews and careful analysis of what non-Christians thought of Christians. Their results were discouraging. Kinnaman wrote, "Our research shows that many of those outside of Christianity, especially younger adults, have little trust in the Christian faith, and esteem for the lifestyle of Christ followers is quickly fading among outsiders."[1]

One of the biggest objections non-Christians had to the Christian faith is that believers are too judgmental. The authors say that to be judgmental "is to point out something that is wrong in someone else's life, making the person feel put down, excluded, and marginalized." How common is it for people to feel that way around Christians? These researchers found that almost "nine out ten young outsiders (87 percent) said that the term *judgmental* accurately describes present-day Christianity."[2]

Christians are often surprised by that perception because they see themselves much more positively. When asked whether their churches "accept and love people unconditionally," 76 percent of pastors strongly agreed, but only 20 percent of outsiders of all ages gave the same answer.[3]

Whenever I have raised the subject of judging with Christians, I have noticed their most common first impulse is to prepare a defensive stance about their own behavior that could be considered judgmental. By contrast, people I talk to outside the church are quick to identify with the judged rather than the ones doing the judging. This distinction is significant. Christians often believe the accusation that they are judgmental is unfair, but maybe their automatic defensiveness about it is an indication that there may be some truth to it, that the dark side of a passionate belief in Christ and Christian values is the temptation to impose a strict code of conduct on everyone and to jump on their flaws when they don't live up to it.

The Pharisees in the Gospel accounts were ardent followers of their faith, but now we mostly think of them not as righteous people but as judgmental people who entirely missed the point of Jesus's teaching. The Christ followers I know don't want to end up that way. What will it mean to live up to Jesus's teaching about not being judgmental? Perhaps the first step is to admit that judging is part of our nature. Judging is our default action, and we are prone to it even if we consciously disavow it.

If you don't think you judge, consider this. I will give you one fact about someone. Think of what first comes to your mind when you picture that person. I present to you a man who has tattoos all over his face. What assumptions about him leap into your thoughts? You know only one fact—tattoos. But do several labels or fears or judgments spring to mind? If you saw him in person, would your natural inclination be to fill in the gaps of your knowledge about him with assumptions of your own? Which would you guess him to be, a stockbroker or an ex-convict? Does he run a daycare center, or does he run with a gang? You don't *know*. You have only one fact. But doesn't your mind want to leap to a few more conclusions?

If you are walking down the sidewalk and see a silver-haired man in a three-piece suit and a few minutes later see a woman hobbling along pushing a shopping cart filled with old clothes and plastic bags, which one do you assume is homeless? For all you *know*, both of them might be homeless, or maybe neither is homeless. Most of us would assume the woman is homeless, but maybe she is pushing the cart toward her home. Maybe the silver-haired man has dressed up to conceal his homeless condition.

These kinds of snap judgments are unavoidable. We are constantly making judgments, some harmless, some not. Just as we constantly fill in gaps about others that go beyond our knowledge, people are also constantly filling in gaps about us. Are you ever frustrated or hurt by the false assumptions people make about you? Maybe your facial expression is judged as bored or grouchy when in fact you're engaged in deep contemplation or active listening. Maybe you're judged as aloof when you're merely shy. Maybe your appearance itself makes people jump to wrong conclusions. I know a man who complains that his face is structured in such a way that when he has a neutral expression, it looks as if he's frowning. He is frequently accused of being in a bad mood when he is content.

Sometimes someone's negative assessment about us may have some validity because we have screwed up, but even then, we hope for mercy rather than harsh judgment. Sometimes I let people down. Sometimes I lose my temper and lash out. I fail to follow through on a commitment. I say something stupid. I fail in dozens of ways. I deserve criticism, maybe even condemnation, but I crave understanding. I hope for a second chance. I did wrong, and I may have to pay consequences for it, but I also long for forgiveness. Maybe in those vulnerable moments, one question I should ask myself is, am I willing to give others the same understanding and forgiveness that I hope and expect from them? *For in the same way you judge others,* Jesus said, *you will be judged, and with the measure you use, it will be measured to you.*

If you are a Christian reading this chapter, you have probably been accused of being judgmental. Instead of reading this chapter only through that lens, I would invite you first to think of a time when *you* were the one harshly judged. Have you felt the sting of that attitude? Have you been treated like the outsider, the one who doesn't fit? Have you wanted to explain your behavior or beliefs but knew you would face a hostile reception? Have you felt misunderstood but also helpless to explain yourself in a way that your unsympathetic judges would understand? Christians do face that kind of judgment sometimes. In order to grasp judgmentalism more fully, it may be helpful to think of this issue from both perspectives—as the judge *and* as the victim of judgment. These roles are not hard to imagine since most of us have played both of them at some point.

Those who are perceived as judgmental may defend their words by saying they are acting out of concern for the person they are correcting. Their concern may be genuine, but think of your own experience with people. Do you feel like taking *any* advice, no matter how sound, from someone you feel is judging you? Most people faced with judgmental attitudes only want to flee to a safe spot. What if the person really does need that advice that the judgmental person wants to give? What if the judged person's life really would be better if they did what the judge is suggesting? Most of us would be willing to hear such words *only* from someone we truly trust—someone who undoubtedly loves us, someone we invite into that intimate sphere, not someone who pushes their way into it. Judgment backfires. Love gets heard.

Social Media as a Toxic Judging Ground

If judging is a bigger problem today than in previous generations, one reason may be that, thanks to social media and other online venues, our lives are more public than ever before. For most people, their photos, political opinions, memories, stray thoughts, and other details of their everyday lives used to be mostly shared with only a small number of people around them. This interaction happened mostly in person, where reactions could be gauged and social customs called for restraint in being too blunt about sensitive issues like politics and religion. Before social media came along, I often knew the political views of only my closest friends. Now, thanks to Facebook and Twitter, I am bombarded daily with the political views of people I knew only casually in high school or met once at a conference or last saw at a family reunion ten years ago. Rarely are these views presented in carefully reasoned paragraphs supported by research and fair-minded analysis. They are far more likely to be exaggerated rants or memes that rely more on emotion than evidence. The comments these posts spawn are often even less thoughtful, mere gut responses to half-baked ideas. Is it any wonder that this system produces hurt feelings, misunderstandings, and tones of judgment?

If you think you can enter into this social media arena and elevate the tone with your own reasonable approach, I invite you to try it. Do you want to post as a Democrat? Republican? Christian? Atheist? I guarantee there is someone out there waiting to judge you—or condemn or threaten or humili-ate or mock you—for it. Do you have opinions on women's rights? Abortion? Sexuality? Prepare to be labeled, stereotyped, and scolded. Some people troll the internet in permanent outrage, castigating whoever crosses their path. Of course, social media can be a place of connection, good humor, fun, helpful information, and stimulating conversation—but it has also done significant harm to relationships and coarsened the judgmental tone many people use toward one another.

It's easy to identify judgmental people on social media or in the com-ments section of just about any publication, but most of us don't think of *our-selves* as judgmental. However, scroll through Facebook or some other social media for a while and see how judgmental you can start to become. Does it drive you crazy how unreasonable people can be, how blind and hypocritical, how twisted in their values? Are you amazed when you read a political post written by someone you used to respect but who is now talking like an idiot? Do you have trouble imagining how someone could come to some of these ridiculous conclusions about social issues or people's rights? Are you tempt-ed to either unfriend them or else drop all your restraint and respond with a comment that will reveal to the world how stupid they are being? When our evaluations of people cause us to want to marginalize them, exclude them, put them down, stereotype them, or take a superior attitude toward them, we are judging them. For many of us, it's hard to spend much time on social media without sliding into that type of behavior. I don't simply disagree with someone's position. I find myself rolling my eyes and wanting to dismiss that person altogether.

What impact does all this online judging have? One thing many of us do to avoid the sting of judgment is to make our lives and ourselves look as good as possible online so that other people have as little ammunition as possible to use against us as they judge us. As Donna Freitas points out in her book *The Happiness Effect*, the rise of social media has made us more defensive about our weaknesses and vulnerabilities than ever. Feeling a little down? Don't post it on social media—people may judge you as a loser! Does a photo make you look fat? Better post a different one that shows you in a more flattering light. Spending the evening alone to read a book and enjoy some solitude? Don't admit it online! People may judge you as friendless. Post a photo of yourself laughing with others instead.

As people self-protectively create an online persona that is happier and more prosperous than their actual lives, others look on and feel more discouraged about their own lives. Many are able to dismiss that comparison and realize that social media is not reality, but some may feel spurred to tear down others in order to make their own lives seem not as bad by comparison. Cyber-bullying has had devastating consequences for young people in particular, leading to depression and even suicide in some cases. One teenage boy featured on NBC's *Today* show became an anti-bullying spokesperson after seeing the pain his own cyber-bullying had on a teenage girl. He was jealous of the friendship she had formed with his own best friend, so he and a group of his friends bullied her by text and telephone, calling her ugly, calling her a troll, and even urging her to commit suicide. She told *Today*, "I felt like my self-confidence was ripped out." She is far from alone, since around 80 percent of students report seeing a classmate get bullied once a week.[4]

Toxic social media affects people of all ages. Commenting on the prevalence of anger on social media, Susanna Schrobsdorff wrote in *Time* magazine that we're "so primed to be mad about something every morning, it's almost disappointing when there isn't an infuriating tweet to share or a bit of our moral turf to defend waiting in our phones."[5] Researchers back her up. Schrobsdorff cites a study of seventy million social media posts that found that anger—more than other emotions, like sadness or joy—was the emotion that caused ideas to spread online most quickly. Anger affects us not only psychologically but also physically, giving us a boost of adrenaline that triggers a fight-or-flight response. Over time, insulting language that once would have been shocking becomes so common that people begin to accept it and ramp up their own language.[6] The fight goes far beyond simple disagreement over issues and becomes an us-versus-them battle that makes us more interested in rhetorically obliterating the enemy than in finding out the truth. People are depersonalized. Rules of polite conversation are set aside. Is it any wonder that people feel judged and misunderstood?

And Yet . . . Judgments Must Be Made

People love to quote the "do not judge" verse when they feel judged themselves, but what did Jesus mean by the statement? He certainly is not saying that his followers should not make judgments about anything. Other parts of the New Testament, including Jesus's own teaching, give guidance for the kinds of judgments that should be made. For example, only a few verses after the "do not judge" passage in Matthew 7, Jesus tells his disciples, "Watch out for false prophets. They come to you in sheep's clothing, but inwardly they are ferocious wolves. By their fruit you will recognize them. Do people pick grapes from thornbushes, or figs from thistles? Likewise, every good tree bears good fruit, but a bad tree bears bad fruit" (vv. 15–17). Recognizing false prophets by their fruit obviously requires judgments to be made.

Several chapters later, when Jesus sends out his disciples to the surrounding towns to minister, he tells them to look "for some worthy person" in the town and stay with them (10:11). Then, "If the home is deserving, let your peace rest on it; if it is not, let your peace return to you. If anyone will not welcome you or listen to your words, leave that home or town and shake the dust off your feet" (vv. 13–14). All those decisions require judgment calls about people. Many other examples could be given, but clearly Jesus wanted disciples who could make decisions using wise discernment.

Jesus does not simply say, "Do not judge" and leave it at that. He follows that with his metaphor of looking at the speck in your brother's eye while not paying attention to the plank in your own. Proper judgment requires humility, in at least two senses. First, we need to remember that we are not perfect and that we have been lavishly forgiven for our own sins. Jesus requires—not only here but also in his teaching in other passages, including the Lord's Prayer and some of his parables—that his followers forgive others as they have been forgiven.

Second, we need to judge humbly because only God is qualified to make ultimate judgments about people. No matter how much indignation we may feel toward someone, we should hold any ultimate judgment lightly because we do not know someone to the depths of their soul the way God does. We do not bear the burden of making any final pronouncement on a person. It's neither our job nor our right.

When I think about when I feel the least judgmental, it is often when I feel the most vulnerable about my own actions. My judgment is most merciful when I am aware of the plank in my own eye. I know people who live—and judge—as if they don't have any planks, but they are fooling themselves. A plank in your eye blinds you, and many go through life blinded by their own planks. I am my most haughty and self-righteous self when I look at someone else and see them as a whole other category of person than I am. Putting them at a distance in that way makes it easier for me to judge them as more sinful, more deserving of condemnation, more disgusting or unworthy than I am. When I get into that mindset, Jesus calls on me to look at the plank in my own eye. Although it is important for us to realize that, when God forgives our sins, they are truly no longer held against us, it is also important to have a constant awareness of how much forgiveness God has poured out on us. We need a healthy sense of our own shortcomings and sins. That's why one of the lines in the Lord's Prayer is, "And forgive us our debts, as we also have forgiven our debtors" (Matthew 6:12). Jesus repeatedly connects our own forgiveness to our willingness to forgive others.

The Pharisees and teachers of the law tried to set a trap for Jesus when they brought him a woman caught in the act of adultery. They wanted to see what he would do about the law that commanded that she be stoned to death. Already, before that question is even discussed, they have failed the test Jesus sets for judgment and forgiveness. Their motivation is not justice. They act not out of a concern for preserving marriages, but merely to enhance their own standing at the expense of the woman, and to tear down a teacher they see as a threat. The woman they drag to him is merely a prop, dehumanized and humiliated (and the man with whom she committed adultery nowhere in sight).

Jesus knows there are some pretty big planks in those eyes that are staring at him and waiting for a decision. He says, "Let any one of you who is without sin be the first to throw a stone at her" (John 8:7). Once they slink away, he talks to the woman as if she is a real human being. Although he is the only man in the group who is truly without sin, he does not choose to use that righteous position to condemn her. His message to her is, "Go now and leave your life of sin" (v. 11).

I have often heard of various forms of gratitude journals, in which people make a list each day of a certain number of things they are grateful for. I have done this myself and have found it to be helpful in changing my perspective to show me how much I have to be thankful for in my life. Maybe people should occasionally keep another kind of journal in which they list the planks in their eyes, such as the bad attitudes or actions or habits they are prone to. Some-one's list could include things such as a bad temper, a tendency to jump to negative conclusions about people, selfishness, greed, and so on.

How would a greater awareness of my planks change the way I judge others? Would I be a little more likely to extend some grace? Such a list of planks should not be used to wallow in sins that have been forgiven; instead, they should offer us an honest look at our own weaknesses and serve as a reminder of all the things for which we have been forgiven, which might push us closer to Jesus's ideal of refraining from taking on a habitual mindset of harsh judgment. One problem, of course, is that the planks can be so blinding that we either are not aware of them at all or we know they're there but don't want to admit it. It takes extraordinary self-awareness to be able to admit to things such as, *I tend to be suspicious of people of certain races,* or, *My envy leads me to behave more harshly toward people who are smarter or more successful or better-looking than I am.*

Not all judging springs from a motivation of arrogant self-righteousness like the men showed when they dragged the woman caught in adultery to Jesus. Often some *good* motives are mixed into a Christian's reasons for judging, which might make it harder to recognize when the Christian is stepping over a line into an unloving mindset that Jesus would challenge. Many Christians desire justice. They want to set the world right. They believe people should behave a certain way and that standards of right and wrong should be upheld. Those motivations are admirable—especially when we focus them on our own behavior. Those motives can also lead to positive change on a larger scale, but as we have seen, they can easily turn toxic when those attitudes morph into superiority, condemnation, or dehumanization. If love is pushed out, we have crossed the line Jesus warned about.

When it comes to Christians confronting people about wrong behavior, the Bible makes a distinction between how we approach fellow Christians and how we handle those outside the church. In Matthew 18:15–19, Jesus outlines a method for handling conflict when a believer sins against a fellow believer. This method emphasizes the desired outcome of reconciliation; it also emphasizes bringing other Christians into the process to provide perspective and support. First, one goes to the offending person on one's own to discuss the problem and work out the differences. If that doesn't work, one brings others into the process. If that doesn't work, one takes the problem to the church itself. Reconciliation may happen at any point in the process, but sometimes it doesn't, and then relationship is broken. That process may sound long and awkward, but it takes the burden of a difficult reconciliation off one person alone. It brings in support from the community of faith, and it is far better than one person lashing out in harsh judgment.

Some Christians are too quick to judge, but others may be too willing to shirk the responsibility for church discipline that the Bible calls for. Either extreme is unscriptural and can lead to devastating consequences. I once was part of the leadership council of a church group that had to confront one of our fellow leaders about his behavior that violated the standards of our group. It was not something so egregious that it demanded his immediate removal, but it wasn't so minor we could overlook it. I didn't want to take part in the process. I had never been placed in such a position and felt embarrassed to have to confront my friend in this way. One of the other leaders urged us not to let it slide, emphasizing the importance of bathing the whole process in prayer so we could approach our friend in an attitude of love and reconciliation. I reluctantly went along, and to my relief, it worked. A week after committing to pray about it, we met with our friend and said we had become aware of some of these behaviors and had to discuss it with him. We affirmed his leadership, his friendship, and his value to us, but also articulated that what he was doing was not acceptable. At first he responded with some eye-rolling and sighs, but as the conversation went on, he accepted what we were saying. The behavior stopped. The friendships survived, and he was able to continue in his role in the group.

Liberated from Judging

Jesus's "do not judge" command is often seen as prohibitive (*I'm not allowed to judge someone*), but another way to look at it is that it is actually liberating (*I don't have to be responsible for monitoring everyone else's behavior; my responsibility is to love*). That is a positive command. God can take care of the judgment. That's his job. In a portion of 1 Corinthians in which Paul is showing the Corinthian church how to deal with a case of immorality within their community, he emphasizes that the disciplinary steps he is calling for apply to fellow believers, not to the world in general. He writes, "What business is it of mine to judge those outside the church? Are you not to judge those inside? God will judge those outside" (5:12–13a).

Christians often go wrong in their zeal to impose Christian behavior on those who are not Christians. It does no good to persuade people merely to behave a certain way if they reject Jesus Christ, the foundation of our faith. Our responsibility is not to get them to act a certain way but, rather, to lead them to Christ. Our message should not be, "Change your behavior." It should be, "Believe in the Lord Jesus, and you will be saved" (Acts 16:31). As a Christian, I'm happy to be free from the responsibility to regulate everyone's actions. Because nonbelievers do not approach the world from a Christian perspective, many of those behavioral prohibitions wouldn't make sense for them anyway.

When my children were little, they were not allowed to punish one another or decide the punishment for each other no matter how much they wanted to. My wife and I would take care of that, thank you. They could love each other all they wanted. They could get along, support one another, or give to one another. That's what we wanted them to do. Even if one of them was being completely naughty and obnoxious, we still didn't want the other sibling to straighten him or her out. Go ahead and continue to be nice to the naughty one, we urged, and we'll handle the bad behavior.

With judging, some Christians worry that not speaking out against someone's sin is tantamount to endorsing it. But just as one child laying down the law and doling out punishment to another within a family would almost certainly lead to trouble—resentment and cries of "You're not the boss of me!"—so the judgment of Christians against those not in the faith causes offense and does nothing to lead anyone to Christ.

Society itself must make judgments about certain kinds of bad behavior, of course—murder, theft, rape, and so on. In the legal arena we have a huge and elaborate system of police, courts, lawyers, juries, lawsuits, and, well, *judges*, to do the judging. That liberates me as an individual from having to monitor all this behavior. I may serve on a jury or call the police if I see a crime taking place, but I don't have to take on myself the duties of searching out possible criminals and deciding their guilt or innocence. Even when I do play a part as a citizen in making a judgment about someone else, such as when I serve as a juror, the judgment is not left solely to me. I will be only one of a *group* of jurors because those who created the system in which I function knew how easy it would be for one person's judgment to be wrong, so they built in checks and balances to increase the chances of getting it right. That system prohibits me as an individual from exacting punishment on someone I think has broken the law. However certain I may feel that someone else has done something illegal, I can't take it upon myself to give them a jail sentence or fine them or physically harm them. Why? Because creators of the legal system realized that my judgment as an individual was too likely to be biased and flawed. Others will need to be brought in to make sure the judgment is fair. If a secular legal system puts in such protections against rash judgment, then shouldn't Christians also be careful about judging in situations that are *not* regulated by law?

What can we do to become less judgmental and live out Jesus's call to pay more attention to the plank in our own eye than the speck in our brother's? There are many specific ways to live out Jesus's command, but they all center on one idea: love. What happens if you approach other people with love rather than judgment? If you love, you may realize that, even if people *deserve* the harsh judgment you are tempted to give them, you are not the one who should give it. Leave that to God. If you love, you will see that you are free from the burden of setting everyone straight. You have certain responsibilities as a church member and a citizen, but even those duties are to be carried out with love and with the support of the church or legal system. You do not have the right or the burden to judge alone, so don't.

If you love, you will focus on fixing your own issues rather than condemning the faults of others. If you love, you will realize you have blind spots. You may not know everything about why people behave the way they do—the pain they are feeling, or the confusion that is pushing them, or the difficult past that has shaped them. Love will give you the humility to realize there may be missing pieces in your understanding. It will allow you to hold off before saying something or posting something or assuming something.

Sometimes in the college literature courses I teach, we study works from writers who hold passionately differing views from one another. Booker T. Washington and W.E.B. DuBois, for example, were African-American leaders of an earlier era who differed significantly on their approaches to racial issues. Washington urged more of a patient, go-slow approach, while DuBois emphasized the need to demand civil rights. One method I use to study these differences is that, after the students have read the works of both men, I split the class into two groups and ask one side to represent Washington and the other side DuBois. I don't let the students choose which group they are assigned to. Some groan when I announce which man they will have to represent, since their own sympathies lie firmly with the other one. Groups are given some time to marshal the best arguments of their assigned man, and then we debate the issues. Students must speak not as themselves but as the man to whom they are assigned. They may quote from his works, but they say, "As I wrote in my book . . ."

This exercise always leads to lively discussion that brings out the key issues, and what fascinates me about it is how quickly students can shift from groaning, eye-rolling opposition to a sincere embrace—or least fair understanding—of those views once they have to articulate the ideas themselves. By being forced to defend ideas from a certain perspective, students begin to see how a particular writer's approach is plausible, even if the student is not ultimately convinced. Some students *are* convinced and switch their own positions through this activity. At the end of the debate, I let students break free from their roles and tell what they really think. It's amazing to see the way most students end up sticking with the man they were assigned.

What if we could somehow apply this approach of seeing through someone else's eyes to our judgments of other people? What if we could truly enter their background and brokenness before we judged them? Would that make their behavior more understandable to us? Sometimes yes, sometimes no. Would it change our harsh response or attitude toward them? It might. To truly enter someone's way of thinking—to take into account their fears, insecurities, prejudices, misunderstandings, limitations, and painful pasts—is a step toward knowing them. Not excusing or rationalizing or enabling or ignoring—but understanding. From understanding, love can grow. The unspoken message at the heart of Jesus's negative command, "Do not judge" is his oft-repeated positive command, "Love one another."

Notes

1. David Kinnaman and Gabe Lyons, *unChristian: What a New Generation Really Thinks about Christianity . . . and Why It Matters* (Grand Rapids: Baker Books, 2007), 11.

2. Kinnaman and Lyons, *unChristian*, 182.

3. Kinnaman and Lyons, *unChristian*, 185.

4. "Bullies Speak: 'We judged her . . . without knowing who she was,'" *TODAYMoms* (blog), *Today*, NBC Universal, October 18, 2012, https://www.today.com/parents/bullies-speak-we -judged-her-without-knowing-who-she-was-1C6539150.

5. Susanna Schrobsdorff, "Viral Anger Spreads Like a Disease—and It's Making the Country Sick," *Time* (July 10/July 17, 2017), 19–20.

6. Schrobsdorff, "Viral Anger," 19–20.

Digging Deeper

1. Why are Christians so often seen as judgmental? Has that been your experience? What can Christians do to change that perception?

2. People use the phrase "do not judge" to mean all kinds of things. How would you describe the essence of how Jesus used that command? What did he *not* mean by it?

3. Some would argue that the rise of social media has brought about an increase in judgmental attitudes and behaviors. Do you agree? What can be done to make social media a less abusive tool?

4. This chapter points out that Jesus required his disciples to make certain judgments about people and issues. What are ways to make the distinction between judging in a harmful way and making necessary judgment calls?

5. The author points out that, even though "do not judge" is often seen as a command that prohibits behavior, not having to judge someone can also be liberating. In what ways is it liberating not to judge people?

Go to https://www.thefoundrypublishing.com/12NT/LeaderGuide for a free downloadable leader's guide that includes more questions for reflection as well as activities for use in a small group setting.

5

The Sermon on the Mount // James Jacques Joseph Tissot // c. 1886-1896

The Lord's Prayer

⁹ This, then, is how you should pray:
"Our Father in heaven, hallowed be your name,
¹⁰ Your kingdom come, your will be done, on earth as it is in heaven.
¹¹ Give us today our daily bread.
¹² And forgive us our debts, as we also have forgiven our debtors.
¹³ And lead us not into temptation, but deliver us from the evil one."

—Matthew 6:9–13

WHEN YOU REACH life's worst, scariest, and most consequential moment, what do you say? What do you pray?

Todd Beamer reached such a horrible moment on September 11, 2001. On that morning, which would become one of the most infamous dates in American history, Beamer boarded United Airlines flight 93 from Newark to San Francisco. His plane would never arrive. Elsewhere that morning, terrorists flew hijacked planes into the Twin Towers of the World Trade Center in New York City, collapsing those buildings and killing thousands. Other conspirators flew a plane into the Pentagon in Washington, DC, killing almost two hundred more people. America was under attack, and no one knew how many more planes might hit what targets or what other horrors might be in store. Across the country, planes were ordered to land and airports closed.

Terrorists also took over Todd's flight that morning, forcing their way into the cockpit and removing the pilot and copilot. Once they had control, they told the passengers they had a bomb and that everyone should stay in their seats. The passengers felt the plane lurch in a different direction. The flight was now headed to Washington, DC. Although the passengers were not allowed to get up, they were not prevented from making phone calls, so many of them called loved ones, knowing it might be for the last time. Todd considered calling his wife but instead hoped such a dire call might not be necessary if he and the others could somehow turn the situation around.[1]

As information from people's calls began to spread around the plane, passengers realized the hijacking of their plane was almost certainly tied to the other attacks against the Pentagon and World Trade Center. What would happen to them? Would their plane be flown into the White House? The Capitol building?

Todd called a GTE Airfone Customer Care operator, who followed a distress-call manual as she led him through a series of questions and took notes on the call. At first some of the passengers thought maybe they would be able to take back the plane from the terrorists and, with help from the ground and from a few men onboard who had some knowledge of flying, somehow figure out how to land safely. That plan did not come to fruition, but Todd and the others were determined not to give up without a fight. No more landmark buildings would be struck that day. Just before he and other passengers rushed the cockpit, Todd asked the operator to tell his wife and sons that he loved them.

For many people, the conversation might have ended there. Todd knew he was staring not only at the scariest moment of his life but also, almost certainly, at the end of his life. He made only one more request.

He asked the operator to recite the Lord's Prayer with him. She did so. Every word.

Why that prayer? Why then?

Todd's wife, Lisa, who wrote about her husband's experience in her book, *Let's Roll! Ordinary People, Extraordinary Courage*, said she had never heard Todd recite that prayer in tough situations, but it didn't surprise her. Their pastor had recently taught a series on the prayer, and Todd kept a bookmark of it in one of his books. The part of the prayer that intrigued Todd the most was the request to forgive us our trespasses as we forgive those who trespass against us. Lisa wrote, "I felt certain that, in some way, Todd was forgiving the terrorists for what they were doing."[2]

After that prayer, Todd said, "Jesus, help me," and he and other passengers rushed the cockpit. They ran the plane into the ground in Pennsylvania, preventing the terrorists from fulfilling whatever horrific mission they had in mind.

The Most Influential Prayer in History

The Lord's Prayer has become the most famous prayer in history. When countless millions of people across the world hear those first few words, "Our Father, who art in heaven," their minds automatically start filling in the rest. Many who recite it may have never actually read it within the Bible itself. Many will not remember ever consciously trying to memorize it; they have the feeling they have always known it. Those of us who learned the prayer in English are most likely to recite it in the King James translation, passed down to us over the generations, even though we may have adopted a more modern translation of the Bible for use in other situations.

The Lord's Prayer has been recited aloud in churches and other gatherings of Christians for centuries, since the time of the early church. Tertullian, in the third century, called it "an abridgement of the entire gospel."[3] In the twentieth century, Archbishop of Canterbury Rowan Williams agreed, writing, "If somebody said, give me a summary of Christian faith on the back of an envelope, the best thing to do would be to write our Lord's Prayer."[4]

Countless other Christian leaders and writers have written about the prayer over the centuries, such as Origen, Dante, Teresa of Avila, Francis of Assisi, Augustine, Thomas Aquinas, Gregory of Nyssa, and many others. The prayer has also been sung and recorded countless times by a wide variety of artists. One popular song version of the prayer was written by Albert Hay Malotte in 1935. That version alone has been recorded by artists as widely varying as LeAnn Rimes, Jackie Evancho, Elvis Presley, Mahalia Jackson, Bill and Gloria Gaither, Yolanda Adams, Perry Como, Susan Boyle, Michael W. Smith, David Phelps, Charlotte Church, Patti LaBelle, Barbra Streisand, Andrea Bocelli, Jose Carreras, Sarafina, Engelbert Humperdinck, Johnny Mathis, George Beverly Shea, Michael Wood, Mario Lanza, Andy Williams, Sandi Patty, Jim Nabors, and many more. What other song—let alone prayer—has attracted the interest of such a wide array of singers? YouTube contains tens of thousands of videos of the song, in many languages.

The Lord's Prayer also makes many appearances in films, even when those movies are not written from a Christian perspective overall. Blogger Dean A. Anderson has written about a long list of films in which someone prays or discusses the prayer. Some films and shows have presented it respectfully, such as *Shane, The Deer Hunter, Master and Commander,* and the HBO series *Deadwood.* Other films have used it negatively or sarcastically, such as *I Heart Huckabees* or *The Two of Us.* Even horror films, such as *The Omen* and *The Seventh Victim,* sometimes include the Lord's Prayer. So do films based on comics, such as *Spider-man* and *X-Men United.* Films based on national tragedies, such as the 9/11 movies *United 93* and *The World Trade Center,* or the BP oil-spill film *Deepwater Horizon,* also show people reciting the prayer.[5]

Easy to Memorize, Harder to Pray

The Lord's Prayer is given particular prominence in the Catholic tradition, but its importance and relevance transcend denominational barriers. The practice of reciting the Lord's Prayer aloud in unison, which happens millions of times each week in churches and other ceremonies across the globe, has made the prayer familiar—but has that practice led to a deeper understanding of it? I am embarrassed to think of how many times I have droned mindlessly through a recitation of the prayer without *really* praying it or without giving a thought to what the words really mean. It's easy to follow its regular rhythms the way we work our way through the phrases of the American pledge of allegiance or the national anthem, parroting the words out of respect but not focusing on what they say.

The Lord's Prayer may be more influential than any other prayer in history, but the danger is that its recitation has become so mechanical that it can also become less meaningful than even the simplest heartfelt prayer, such as, "Thank you, God!" or, "Help!" Certainly there can be good reasons to recite a familiar prayer, even when circumstances don't allow us to intently focus on every word or phrase. This recitation can have the same benefits as singing a familiar song. When we sing a worship song or hymn that we love, it connects us not only to the worship that is happening in that particular moment but also to our memories and feelings and experiences of all the other times we have sung the song. It also is a way of connecting us to all those around us who are singing it and, perhaps, to other believers in other times and places who have sung it. In that sense, singing a favorite song, even when we are not consciously aware of the meaning of every word every time we sing it, is an even more powerful experience than singing a new song. We keep learning new songs, but we don't stop singing or reciting old songs simply because we already know them so well. The repetition—and the experience it evokes—is part of the joy of singing.

So it can be with repeating the Lord's Prayer. It connects us with other believers in unified petition to the Father. When we pray it in times of crisis or stress, such as when Todd Beamer prayed it on United flight 93, it connects us to our faith and to our Lord immediately, just as familiar greetings connect us to friends and loved ones even if those greetings are not new or creative. When my wife arrives home at the end of a day of work, I often greet her with a kiss and a phrase like, "Hi, honey!" Not too original or creative, is it? But connection, not complexity of ideas, is what that moment of reconnection calls for.

Recitation may serve those positive purposes, but Jesus did not teach the prayer as an incantation to be repeated word for word in order to produce some kind of magic effect. It's helpful to consider why he taught the prayer in the first place. The prayer appears in two places in the Bible—in Matthew and in Luke. The version that is most often memorized and recited is the longer version found in Matthew. But the Luke version says that one day "Jesus was praying in a certain place. When he finished, one of his disciples said to him, 'Lord, teach us to pray, just as John taught his disciples'" (11:1).

The disciples asked for prayer instruction after watching Jesus pray. How should one approach the Father? What issues are appropriate to bring to him? When Jesus offers his prayer, he is saying, do something like this, or, let me give you an example. Nothing in Matthew or Luke indicates he was limiting their prayers to only these phrases and ideas. Certainly Jesus himself, in the prayers recorded in Scripture, moved beyond *only* these words and topics. But to have a robust prayer life, this is how to approach the Father in prayer each day.

In Matthew, the prayer appears as part of the Sermon on the Mount. Jesus teaches his followers not to use prayer as a tool to make themselves look pious or to show off. "Do not be like the hypocrites," he says, "for they love to pray standing in the synagogues and on the street corners to be seen by others" (Matthew 6:5). Take prayer seriously. Go in your room and shut the door and truly pray to God, not to some audience who may be watching you. He adds, "And when you pray, do not keep on babbling like pagans, for they think they will be heard because of their many words. Do not be like them, for your Father knows what you need before you ask him" (vv. 7–8). Prayer, then, is not about getting the words right or impressing someone else or repeating the prayer so many times that God answers it just to get you off his back. Only with those warnings in mind does Jesus then give them the prayer on which they can model their own prayers.

The Essence of Prayer

One way to think of the Lord's Prayer is that it is prayer boiled down to its essence. If you had to break down regular, daily prayer to its most basic level, in which nothing could be deleted without real loss, you would have the prayer Jesus modeled for his disciples. The prayer shows us what is important, what we should focus on, what matters.

Those who learn to follow the contours of this prayer in their own prayer lives may be surprised how it shakes up their usual patterns of thought and action. When it is recited in public settings, it may come across as stiff, full of nice sentiments about daily bread and forgiveness. But those who take the words seriously and truly pray them may find that concepts such as inviting the coming of the kingdom of God and forgiving our debtors are more disruptive than they first imagined.

Is this a prayer you really want to pray? Before you pray it, consider what it means.

Our Father in Heaven

The "our" in this prayer should not be taken lightly. Think of who is praying that word. Jesus, approaching the Father, does not say "my" Father. He includes *us* in the prayer. The very reason Jesus came to Earth was to create a bridge for us to reach the Father, and in this prayer he is doing it. When we pray, we approach the Father with Jesus.

"Our" also makes clear that the entire prayer is more than simply an individualistic prayer to satisfy our own needs. When we pray for daily bread, or forgiveness, or the coming of the kingdom of God, we pray it for all of us. Jesus, by not simply teaching the prayer but also praying it with us, changes our relationship to God from what it would otherwise be. We approach the Father not in our own standing but because Jesus has made it possible.

When Jesus prays to our Father "in heaven," or, in the familiar King James phrase, "who art in heaven," what is his purpose? In one sense, it sounds odd to address God by mentioning where he is. It would be like me speaking to my wife in the next room and saying, "Hey, Peggy, who is in the living room, may I ask you something?" Of course the Father knows where he is, so addressing God in that way must be a reminder to us of *who* he is. We are approaching the Creator of the universe, the Almighty God. We are praying to a God who is far beyond us—not because of his location but because of his identity.

The phrase "Father in heaven," then, contains two ideas about God. Jesus's term for Father is "Abba," which is an intimate term for father. It emphasizes his closeness to us, his loving care. Abba is not an aloof father too mighty and busy and powerful to care about the likes of us. Like a loving earthly father who cares about his children, Abba doesn't expect us to try to approach him as an equal. As we come to him the way a trusting child comes to a loving father, we know he's bigger, smarter, and more powerful than us, but we also know he is on our side. He loves us. He'll use that power to protect us, not to harm us or outdo us.

He is an intimate Father, but he is also a Father "in heaven," which emphasizes all of those majestic qualities we would expect from the Being who not only brought *us* into being but who also created our billions of brothers and sisters and the very planet we live on and the vast expanse of the universe beyond our imagination. As Pierre Raphael puts it, "heaven" in this context "is not a material place; it is beyond everything and contains everything because it is God himself. The reality of God is called heaven. The fullness of life is there, far fuller than on earth. It is a place of joy and of peace, where each of us can find what is most desired."[6] Albert Haase quotes 1 Timothy 6:16, which says that God "lives in unapproachable light." God is too big to be contained in a particular place. Haase writes, "God is indescribable, ineffable, unfathomable, incomprehensible. God is like the air we breathe: we can never grasp it in our hands."[7]

So in one sense we have the indescribability of God, his bigness so beyond us we can't comprehend him ("who art in heaven"), while at the same time, paradoxically, he is "our Abba," as close to us as the most loving Father could be. This is the God to whom we pray.

Hallowed Be Your Name

The *first* thing Jesus requests in his prayer is that the Father's name be revered and adored. Why is the phrase "hallowed be your name" a request rather than a statement? Theology professor Telford Work points out that the church is the instrument God has chosen to "hallow God's name" in the world. Is the church up to such a task? "A world enslaved to mistaken, idolatrous, and even murderous theological apprehensions seems to be too great a challenge for such a frail, divided, compromised community as the church of Jesus Christ," writes Work. "And it is! *That is why the Lord's Prayer is a prayer!*" He says the church cannot accomplish the hallowing of God's name on its own. "We beg for it as a gift we can receive in faith by grace."[8]

"Hallowed be your name," like some of the other lines in the prayer, is both a request and a vision of what will be. *Your kingdom come! Hallowed be your name!* These things *are* happening and *will* happen, and we ask the Father to show us how to participate in their manifestation, how to live into the hope and vision of their reality, and how to keep our minds on these purposes rather than on more trivial matters. The prayer is a plea that God will help us know how to wrap our identity in him.

Your Kingdom Come

Jesus came to Earth to usher in the kingdom of God. Tim Stafford, who writes eloquently about the kingdom of God, explains that the kingdom is not a set of theological propositions but a story. It is an event. "Call it the Jesus event," he says. "Jesus's life was the turning point in the history of Israel, in the history of the world, and in the history of every human being."[9] When Jesus in other places in Scripture says that the kingdom of God is "at hand" or "near," he is saying that it is in progress, that he is now announcing it and ushering it in, and that it will continue through eternity.

Jesus focused his teaching on the kind of kingdom he was bringing to life. Think of how many of his stories begin with "The kingdom of God is like." The Beatitudes and the Sermon on the Mount revealed what the kingdom values would be. His very life, death, and resurrection solidified the saving transformation his kingdom would bring to the world. The coming of the Holy Spirit at Pentecost started to push that kingdom to the ends of the earth, and today, we who are members of that kingdom continue its work. *Your kingdom come!* We have a part to play in the spreading of the kingdom, but we have a constant need to draw on God's power to do it.

How well has the prayer been answered over the years? Stafford says that, in one sense, it's easy for people to scoff at this kingdom. "How much real power does this 'kingdom' possess," he asks, "compared to the forces of the marketplace, compared to the powers of governments, compared to the forces of nature?" On the other hand, at the end of Jesus's life, he had about 120 followers. Today he has more than two billion followers in every part of the globe.[10]

Your Will Be Done, on Earth as it Is in Heaven

Truly praying for God's will to be done is harder than most of us would admit. Instead, I am often tempted to essentially pray, *"My* will be done if I can talk God into cooperating with it." As Christians, even though deep down we know God loves us fully and therefore wants only what is best for us in the long run, we still often have the natural inclination to push back against his will and want to do things our own way because our perspective is limited. We simply don't know what he knows. The "as it is in heaven" phrase in this prayer is a reminder that the Father's perspective is not only beyond us but also beyond Earth itself. It is eternal. He sees the big picture. What we think his will *should* be may seem clear to us, but that may be because we don't know what information we are missing. Will we trust God to lead us into cooperating with his will, even when it seems counterintuitive to our own?

For Jesus, the *will* of God was closely connected to the phrase that precedes this line in the prayer: the *kingdom* of God. Since this is not an individualized prayer, it is a mistake to oversimplify the issue of God's will by reducing it to merely how his will operates in the details of our individual, personal lives—what opportunities we should pursue, jobs we should take, relationships we should cultivate. What if our focus in prayer was instead on his will concerning the kingdom of God? *Your kingdom come, your will be done.* What if our daily tasks and big decisions were geared toward whatever is best for building that kingdom rather than merely getting ahead in the world or winning the competitions of life or burnishing our image? That shift of perspective won't happen automatically. Most people are too selfish by nature. That's why we have to pray it.

Stafford says that he has heard people object to including the phrase "if it is in your will" in their prayers because it sounded too much like fatalism or a lack of faith. However, he believes the phrase can be seen in a different way, representing something beyond personal happiness. Instead of putting ourselves at the center of reality, we put God there, knowing that he "is working to bring the entire cosmos to a good end. The way to that end goes through many dark passages; it involves suffering and pain as well as healing and joy. We do not see clearly how God is leading. Nevertheless we want to place our lives at the center of this great God-centered activity, over and above our own short-sighted interests."[11]

Give Us Today Our Daily Bread

We depend on God for everything, from our spiritual salvation to our most basic physical needs. Even if we do not acknowledge God, he is still the ultimate source of all we have. The words "today" and "daily" are significant in this line of the prayer. Jesus doesn't pray for enough bread to last for the next five years. He asks only for a one-day supply. What about tomorrow? If we are praying to God regularly and keeping intimate contact with him as we should, then we can ask him for tomorrow's bread, tomorrow. When my kids were little and got hungry, they asked for food. Never did they ask what we would feed them a month from now. They trusted it would be there when the time came.

In Exodus, when the Israelites were on their way to the Promised Land, God rained down bread called manna on them every day. They were specifically ordered not to hoard it for the next day. When some disobeyed and saved some extra bread anyway, it became infested with maggots and smelled bad. When Jesus speaks of "bread," he refers not only to bread in particular but also to all the rest of our physical needs. Do we go to him regularly to ask him to fill those needs and to thank him for his physical care of us? Or do we try to arrange our lives so that we are so seemingly self-sufficient that we live as if God has nothing to do with the good things we have received?

The prayer asks God to give "our" daily bread, not "my" daily bread. We are to pray that *all of us* have enough to eat, not just ourselves—even if that means I share part of my portion with those in need. Am I hoarding all the bread while others go hungry? If I enjoy an overabundance, can I authentically pray this prayer without sharing from my wealth in ways that will help the prayer to be answered? In the world in which we live, some go hungry while others have more than they need or could ever use. That's why this *prayer* for daily bread is needed. Not only does Jesus want us to pray it, but the Father may also require us to act as part of fulfilling it. The way he answers the prayer for someone else's bread may be through us.

Throughout the Gospels, when Jesus speaks of bread, he often uses it to symbolize spiritual sustenance. In John 6:35 he says, "I am the bread of life." In Matthew 16, Jesus's disciples think he is scolding them for forgetting to bring bread when he tells them to be on guard against the yeast of the Pharisees and Sadducees. When we pray each day for bread, it is wise to pray not only that God will keep us from physical hunger but also that he will prevent our spiritual starvation.

And Forgive Us Our Debts, as We also Have Forgiven Our Debtors

Marcus Doe survived for years on fantasies of revenge. Living in war-torn Liberia as an eleven-year-old child, he had already lost his mother to illness and now faced each day the possibility of his own death and that of family members. His father worked for the country's corrupt president, who was under attack by rebels trying to overthrow him. For a while, Marcus lived with his older brother behind enemy lines, with little food, no schooling, and constant fear. Even though Marcus and his brother eventually made it to nearby Ghana, his father was not so fortunate. He was killed by rebel forces.

Marcus eventually came to the United States with his brother and his wife, but it was not a happy new beginning. He couldn't focus on creating a new life in America because he was eaten up with fantasies of revenge against the man who had killed his father. Then, when Marcus's brother almost died, he entered the darkest moments of his life.

Fortunately, that is when he turned to God. He says, "I realized, in that darkness, that I could keep those fantasies alive, or I could relinquish them once and for all. I begged God to forgive me. I would let go of revenge and rage." Even with that commitment, it took years for Marcus to learn to forgive his father's killer. He even sought out a meeting with the man but learned that he had been killed in the war. Marcus forgave him anyway, and finally, he says, he could live in peace.[12]

Forgiveness means freedom. Our spiritual survival depends on our willingness to receive forgiveness for ourselves and extend it to others. When it comes to asking God to forgive our debts—or trespasses, or sins—it is easy to err on opposite ends of the spectrum. On one end, we may deny that we have anything to be forgiven for. "This is just the way I am," we may say. We blame others for what we have done.

He provoked me to do it.

It's her fault.

If God didn't want me to be this way, he should have created me differently.

It's God's fault.

There is no such thing as sin. People just do what they do, and it's pointless to feel guilty about it.

Asking for forgiveness is weakness.

He deserved what I did to him.

If I had it to do over again, I'd do it again.

Pierre Raphael—who was a prison chaplain at Rikers Island (New York City's penal colony) for sixteen years and has written a book on the Lord's Prayer—knew many prisoners who, no matter how horrible their crimes, had a hard time seeing any need to be forgiven. For them, the first step toward God's forgiveness was simply the ability to feel remorse. Raphael explains, "The consciences of these people have been anesthetized because of misdeeds too often repeated. Their ability to judge themselves soundly has been killed, and they no longer even think they can be forgiven."[13]

In order to pray, "Forgive us our sins," we must believe first that we *have* sinned, and second, that forgiveness is possible. Some people may need prayer and the intervention of the Holy Spirit to reach those conclusions. When I was growing up in the church, people often spoke of the Holy Spirit "convicting" them of sin. I don't hear that terminology much anymore, but the spiritual concept is real. The Holy Spirit can reveal to us the sin in our lives—not so we wallow in it but so we can know our need for forgiveness and turn to God to ask for it.

If denial of the need to be forgiven is at one end of a destructive spectrum, then at the other end is the false idea that our sins are so egregious that we should not receive forgiveness for them. We can't forgive ourselves, so we don't see how God could forgive us. We don't even want to ask. We may try to make up for this lack of forgiveness by punishing ourselves, or we may shut down spiritually and shut out God.

Any of those responses leads to spiritual death. "Forgive us our sins," Jesus prays. Forgiveness is possible. Jesus prays this just as simply and directly as he prays a request like, "Give us our daily bread." There is no sense of the need to grovel, to beg, to bargain, to agonize. God is willing—and also eager—to forgive as we ask. He does not dangle forgiveness hopelessly out of reach. He offers it. We only have to ask. Like the father in the prodigal son parable, God is running *toward us* to forgive. He is not putting the burden on us to find a way to persuade him why we *deserve* forgiveness. We *don't* deserve it. God offers it anyway because of his tremendous love for us.

As we experience the extravagance of God's love in his forgiveness of us, he expects us—with his help—to offer that same undeserved forgiveness to others. It is hard to do that, so Jesus includes it in his prayer. One thing that makes forgiveness hard in some cases is that the desire not to forgive does not always come only from a stubborn or unloving heart. Sometimes it also springs from a genuine desire to see justice carried out. The trespass that has been committed against us may truly be wrong. It may truly deserve punishment. The person who commits it may do so with no sense of remorse or reluctance. The person may commit the evil with glee. Everything within us cries out for this wrong to be avenged.

This was the problem Jonah faced when God told him to go to Nineveh to preach repentance to the people. He didn't want to preach repentance because he was afraid the people might actually repent—and that God would forgive them! He couldn't stand it. They were truly horrible people, guilty of terrible crimes. Jonah refused to obey God and instead took off in exactly the opposite direction from where God wanted him to go.

The problem is, Jonah thought he knew better than God. If God couldn't see that these people should not be forgiven, then Jonah would have to take matters into his own hands and run away from his assignment to preach repentance so that the people never *would* think to repent and be forgiven.

However, God was determined to offer the chance to repent. He was determined to extend forgiveness and to teach Jonah to preach in a way that might lead to it. After a three-day detour through the belly of a great fish, Jonah did preach to Nineveh, and they did repent, but Jonah still wasn't happy about it.

Jonah is somewhat like the older brother in the prodigal son parable who doesn't think it's fair that the father so readily forgives and embraces and celebrates the younger son who has come home. God has been generous and patient with Jonah, and the father in the prodigal son parable has treated the older brother well his whole life, with the promise of even more love to come. Still, the older brother balks at this generosity being extended to his transgressing sibling, and Jonah pouts about the Ninevites being forgiven.

Jonah and the prodigal son's older brother may seek their own form of justice, but punishment for sin is not their responsibility. In a similar way, when someone commits a murder or theft in our day, there is a legal system in place to determine justice. Individuals are not allowed to take justice into their own hands because they are not impartial enough to determine it fairly. When it comes to personal transgressions against us, the legal system may or may not get involved, depending on what the offense is, but what God calls for us to do is forgive.

Jesus's prayer asks God to forgive us as we forgive others. He links the two. But what about justice? Does God not care about it? Of course he does. He will bring it. *It is his, not ours, to bring about.* We can forgive because we can trust God to bring about justice when and how he sees fit. He will do a much better job with that than we ever could. He takes that burden off us. Our job is to forgive. Let go. Move forward. We must ask God's help to forgive just as urgently—and as often—as we ask him to give us our daily bread.

And Lead Us Not into Temptation, but Deliver Us from the Evil One

As every phrase of this prayer has made clear, Jesus is not praying about concerns we will confront only once every few years or two or three times in a lifetime. He prays for the concerns and threats we face every day—physical needs, the work of the kingdom of God, the need to forgive and be forgiven. Two of the constant threats with which we contend are temptation and evil, not only individually but also as a community of believers. Deliver *us*, the prayer says. Our church. Our community. Our neighborhood. Our family. Our nation. Our world. Have you been part of an organization, city, or other group that is consumed by evil? Have you seen how evil debilitates and sours even the best of intentions in such a community? Deliver us, Lord!

I do lots of praying, but rarely do I think to pray for the Lord to deliver us from evil. This complacency is unwarranted. We live in a world suffused with evil. We are most in danger of it when we least think of it. If the danger of evil rarely crosses our minds, maybe that is because we are already giving in to it, subtly and without our full awareness. Perhaps praying *regularly* for deliverance from evil is one way to at least make us aware of it. Do we *see* injustice, cruelty, exploitation, nastiness, meanness, indifference? Or is it easier to block out all that as we pursue our individual agendas? Certainly those agendas themselves are not necessarily evil, and may even be good: raising our families, paying the bills, surviving. But self-absorption *is* dangerous, if we begin to believe that self-survival is all that matters. To think that evil can't touch us, or that it is someone else's problem, is the best way to inadvertently invite it in.

The Lord's Prayer is often discussed and recited so politely, if not robotically. But phrases like "deliver us from the evil one," if truly prayed, remind us that Christians are in a nonstop spiritual battle. Evil surrounds us. We are under attack. We need to be delivered from evil, and we cannot perform that delivery without God's intervention.

Temptation is the weapon the enemy uses against us in this battle. Temptation itself is not an evil for which we should feel guilty. Jesus was tempted. We are told he was tempted after spending forty days fasting in the desert, and he no doubt faced it at other times that were not recorded. He was in a battle, and he expected it. He prepared for it, which is no doubt why he mentions temptation in his prayer.

A battle is a test, and our victory is possible but not assured. The choice will be ours. Pierre Raphael describes temptation that leads to sin as "a mirage concealing a chasm. It is an attraction that is followed by an emptiness, sometimes by disgust and, in the best of cases, by remorse."[14] Why would remorse be the best of cases? Because remorse at least means that our hearts have not been hardened to the sin we have committed. We still know it is sin, and we still can ask forgiveness for it and be saved from it. Evil, whether it has been let loose in our individual lives or in our community of faith, is a corrosive force that prevents the kingdom of God from being established in our midst. We must fight it constantly—through prayer *and* action.

The Lord's Prayer contains relatively few words, but it can be life-giving if we truly pattern our prayer lives after it. No wonder it has been recited billions of times and memorized perhaps more than almost any other words ever written. It really does contain the gospel message within it. The prayer Jesus taught his disciples has changed the world, and it can change us if we let it.

Notes

1. Lisa Beamer with Ken Abraham, *Let's Roll! Ordinary People, Extraordinary Courage* (Carol Stream, IL: Tyndale House Publishers, 2002), 184–187, 196, 203.

2. Beamer, *Let's Roll!*, 213.

3. Tertullian, "On Prayer," in *Tertullian: Disciplinary, Moral, and Ascetical Works*, trans. Rudolf Arbesmann, Sr. Emily Joseph Daly, and Edwin Quain, vol. 40 of *The Fathers of the Church* (New York: Fathers of the Church, 1959), 159. Quoted in Albert Haase, *Living the Lord's Prayer: The Way of the Disciple* (Downers Grove, IL: IVP Books), 2009, 13–14.

4. Rowan Williams, "The Lord's Prayer," BBC, August 6, 2009, http://www.bbc.co.uk/religion/religions/christianity/prayer/lordsprayer_1.shtml. Quoted in Haase, *Living the Lord's Prayer*, 14.

5. Dean A. Anderson, "The Lord's Prayer in Movies," *Dean A. Anderson* (blog), November 7, 2007, http://deanaanderson.blogspot.com/2007/11/lords-prayer-in-movies.html.

6. Pierre Raphael, *God behind Bars: A Prison Chaplain Reflects on the Lord's Prayer* (New York: Paulist Press, 1999), 19.

7. Haase, *Living the Lord's Prayer*, 62.

8. Telford Work, *Ain't Too Proud to Beg: Living through the Lord's Prayer* (Grand Rapids: William B. Eerdmans Publishing Company, 2007), 45.

9. Tim Stafford, *Surprised by Jesus: His Agenda for Changing Everything in A.D. 30 and Today* (Downers Grove, IL: IVP Books, 2006), 21, 72–73.

10. Stafford, *Surprised by Jesus*, 226, 224.

11. Stafford, *Surprised by Jesus*, 142–43.

12. Marcus Doe, "Why I Forgave the Man I Once Plotted to Kill," *Christianity Today*, October 21, 2016, https://www.christianitytoday.com/ct/channel/utilities/print.html?type=article&id=136305.

13. Raphael, *God behind Bars*, 82.

14. Raphael, *God behind Bars*, 96.

Digging Deeper

1. How familiar is the Lord's Prayer to you? If someone starts to recite it, can you automatically fill in the rest? Can you think of films, songs, ceremonies, or other places where you have heard or seen it used? Of all the prayers that exist, why do you think this one has been so influential?

2. Does the familiarity of this prayer make it *more* meaningful or less? Why do people sometimes choose to recite a familiar prayer rather than praying a new one of their own? In what ways can the prayer be misused?

3. As you consider the various phrases of the prayer, such as, "your kingdom come," or "your will be done," or "as we forgive our debtors," which of the outcomes seem most beyond us without God's direct intervention through prayer?

4. This chapter points out that the Lord's Prayer is not an individualized prayer but is a prayer for *us*. As you look at the specific phrases of the prayer, what implications are there for the fact that you are not only praying for yourself but also for a far wider community?

Go to https://www.thefoundrypublishing.com/12NT/LeaderGuide for a free downloadable leader's guide that includes more questions for reflection as well as activities for use in a small group setting.

6

Christ and Nicodemus, St John, III // English School // 19th century

New Birth

³ *Jesus replied, "Very truly I tell you, no one can see the kingdom of God unless they are born again."*

⁴ *"How can someone be born when they are old?" Nicodemus asked. "Surely they cannot enter a second time into their mother's womb to be born!"*

⁵ *Jesus answered, "Very truly I tell you, no one can enter the kingdom of God unless they are born of water and the Spirit.* ⁶ *Flesh gives birth to flesh, but the Spirit gives birth to spirit.* ⁷ *You should not be surprised at my saying, 'You must be born again.'* ⁸ *The wind blows wherever it pleases. You hear its sound, but you cannot tell where it comes from or where it is going. So it is with everyone born of the Spirit."*

¹⁶ *For God so loved the world that he gave his one and only Son, that whoever believes in him shall not perish but have eternal life.* ¹⁷ *For God did not send his Son into the world to condemn the world, but to save the world through him.* ¹⁸ *Whoever believes in him is not condemned, but whoever does not believe stands condemned already because they have not believed in the name of God's one and only Son.* ¹⁹ *This is the verdict: Light has come into the world, but people loved darkness instead of light because their deeds were evil.* ²⁰ *Everyone who does evil hates the light, and will not come into the light for fear that their deeds will be exposed.* ²¹ *But whoever lives by the truth comes into the light, so that it may be seen plainly that what they have done has been done in the sight of God.*

—John 3:3–8, 16–21

WHAT WOULD IT TAKE to generate 94 million Google searches of one Bible verse during one football game? Heisman trophy-winning quarterback Tim Tebow found out on January 8, 2009, when he wrote "John 3:16" in his eye black during a highly rated championship game. That single biblical recommendation by a prominent Christian athlete, which he made without uttering a word, put this most famous of verses into the minds of tens of millions of football fans.[1]

That was far from the first time this verse has shown up in sporting events. Signs with John 3:16 written on them can often be found scattered throughout the stands at major sporting events. The verse is so well known that the numbers alone, 3:16, have gained their own significance. In fact, as strange as it may sound, World Wrestling Entertainment (WWE) has even managed to legally *trademark* the designation 3:16. WWE's interest in the numbers goes back to 1996, when wrestler Stone Cold Steve Austin competed against Jake Roberts, who was a Christian. In his "King of the Ring" speech after a match, Austin mocked Roberts and his Christian beliefs, saying that his quoting of John 3:16 and other passages of Scripture had done nothing to help Roberts achieve victory. He coined the term "Austin 3:16," and soon after that, the slogan began to appear on signs and other memorabilia, including a shirt that WWE called "the most popular garment of all time."[2] Now WWE plans to sell shirts that include the city name of various matches followed by the 3:16 designation, such as "Los Angeles 3:16."

Other companies also feature 3:16 on their products. In-N-Out Burger, one of the most popular hamburger chains on the west coast, prints "John 3:16" on the bottom of each soda cup. It includes other Scripture references on milkshake cups and burger wrappers. Clothing company Forever 21 also prints "John 3:16" on its shopping bags. Both companies do so as a representation of the faith of their owners or founders.

Neither of these companies print the actual words of the verse on any of their products. The burger eater or clothing buyer would have to look up the verse to discover its content, and the wrestling fan would have to trace the history of "3:16" back to its biblical source. The "3:16" was not even part of the original text of Scripture, of course. The verse and chapter designations were added much later. But they are now shorthand for a message so powerful that people across the world and in various walks of life want to latch onto it, even if, in some cases, they only want to twist it for their own purposes.

Few verses of the Bible so clearly and succinctly confront the most crucial questions of life: *What will save me? Who will rescue me? Where does ultimate meaning reside?*

Jesus Receives a Late-Night Visitor

Maybe such questions were on the mind of Nicodemus—a member of the Sanhedrin, the Jewish ruling council—on the night he came to talk to Jesus. Their conversation leads up to the renowned John 3:16, and the words that surround that verse are no less earth-shattering in their significance for what will be required for ultimate spiritual rescue.

Nicodemus certainly got more than he bargained for when he came to Jesus for this conversation. Some have suggested that the reason he came at night was to avoid the trouble he might get into with his fellow Pharisees by speaking to someone like Jesus, who was, as Murray J. Harris puts it, "a wandering teacher who lacked formal training and who hailed from Galilee in the obscure far north—of all places!"[3] On the other hand, the night is quiet, a good time to have a serious, private conversation. Nicodemus started out politely, but Jesus immediately raised the stakes as high as he possibly could—to ultimate matters of eternal life and death.

Nicodemus started with a compliment, saying that everyone knows Jesus must have come from God because no one could do the miracles he has done otherwise. If Nicodemus was expecting a simple "thank you" for that statement, he was in for a surprise. Instead, Jesus answered with one of the most memorable sentences in history: "Very truly I tell you, no one can see the kingdom of God unless they are born again" (John 3:3). Another way the words can be translated is "born from above." Either way, it wasn't the response Nicodemus expected, and at first, he didn't understand. He had a few questions, and who could blame him? Born again? Once you're old? What was Jesus talking about?

Jesus pushed a little deeper. Emphasizing for the second time the seriousness of what he was conveying to Nicodemus, Jesus began his answer with "Very truly I tell you," and then he said that "no one can enter the kingdom of God unless they are born of water and the Spirit. Flesh gives birth to flesh, but the Spirit gives birth to spirit. You should not be surprised at my saying, 'You must be born again'" (vv. 5–7). However, Nicodemus *was* surprised.

Nicodemus would not have expected to need anything else in order to enter the kingdom of God. He was already a member of the most favored group: the Jews, God's chosen people. And within that group, he was in one of the top, most respected leadership positions. He was set! He was an insider, a good man, a member of a group that wanted to carefully obey religious law to the tiniest degree—yet now Jesus was telling him that wasn't enough? He needed to be "born again"? He needed some kind of complete transformation? He needed a rebirth that would have to come from outside himself, that he could not bring about by his own effort?

Nicodemus was likely to be not only surprised by Jesus's words but also offended. Jesus was directing his words to Nicodemus personally and also to all the people Nicodemus represented. One commentator, Frederick Dale Bruner, even uses the word "shocked" rather than "surprised" in his translation of verse 7. Here is Bruner's translation, which emphasizes the significance of when the "you" is singular or plural: "Please do not be shocked, [Nicodemus], that I said to you [singular, *soi*], 'It is absolutely necessary [dei] that you folks [plural, *hymas*] be born all over again from above.'"[4] Bruner further explains, "The offense of Jesus's remark is heightened when we realize that it is said *to a person* (see the initial *singular* addressee) who believed he had already been born (and biblically circumcised) into the people of God, and that it is said to him *about a people* (see the suddenly *plural* 'you') who believed that they already were, by birth and heritage, the people of God."[5]

Jesus's Words Still Offend—and Save

Many people today are also offended by the idea that they need spiritual rebirth. "I'm fine just the way I am," they claim. "I'm a good person. I have good-enough motives and kind actions and correct views, so no one needs to rescue me." Some might believe that they *are* sinners but still don't need rebirth because they think it isn't necessary ("this is just the way I am"), or they think it isn't possible ("people never really change, so it's useless to think you can be spiritually born again").

A recent study by LifeWay Research showed that most people—67 percent of them, in fact—believe they are sinners and are not happy about it. Only 5 percent of respondents reported not minding being a sinner. You might think that with all that awareness of sin, people would be eager for the new birth Jesus is talking about. However, even though two-thirds of people think they're sinners, far fewer—just 28 percent—believe Jesus is the answer to that problem. A larger number, 34 percent, rely on themselves to take care of their sin problem. They agree with the statement, "I am a sinner, and I work on being less of one."[6]

In his talk with Nicodemus, Jesus denies the self-help option as a way of being rescued from sin and entering the new and eternal life of the kingdom of God he is establishing. You can't give birth to yourself. The first time you were born, physically, you had nothing to do with it. With your spiritual birth, the only part you play is to consent to enter into it through faith. Jesus is not offering any other options. He tells Nicodemus, "No one has ever gone into heaven except the one who came from heaven—the Son of Man. Just as Moses lifted up the snake in the wilderness, so the Son of Man must be lifted up, that everyone who believes may have eternal life in him" (vv. 13–15). With this reminder of the story of Moses lifting up the snake so the people who had been bitten by poisonous snakes could look at it and not die, Jesus is foreshadowing the cross on which he would be lifted up, sacrificing himself so that those who look to him can live eternally.

New birth, or entering the innocence of childhood, is an image Jesus used in other parts of his teaching also. "Truly I tell you, unless you change and become like little children, you will never enter the kingdom of heaven," he says in Matthew 18:3. Henri Nouwen, in his book on the prodigal son parable, points out that when the rebellious son returned home, he considered coming back as a hired servant, but that was unacceptable to the father. His father would accept him only as a son. Nouwen comments, "Receiving forgiveness requires a total willingness to let God be God and do all the healing, restoring, and renewing. If I want to do even a part of that myself, I end up with partial solutions, such as becoming a hired servant. As a hired servant, I can still keep my distance, still revolt, reject, strike, run away, or complain about my pay."[7]

Being born again means *trusting* God to remake us spiritually in ways we could never accomplish on our own. As Nouwen puts it, "Jesus does not ask me to remain a child but to become one. Becoming a child is living toward a second innocence: not the innocence of the newborn infant, but the innocence that is reached through conscious choices."[8] We invite this new birth as a gift from God, but we cannot manufacture it for ourselves.

Wind, Spirit, Light

"Wind" and "Spirit" are the same word in Greek, and Jesus speaks of the Spirit as being like the wind in that it "blows wherever it pleases," and you don't know where it came from or where it is going. This image offers the same kind of challenge to us as the idea of "new birth." Are we willing to allow God to rebirth us? Are we willing to allow the powerful and unpredictable Spirit to blow through our lives and make everything new? That sounds inviting in one sense but potentially disruptive in another. Just when we have everything arranged the way we like it, or at least can live with it, here comes the Spirit to push us in an entirely new direction, to make us feel the sting of guilt over un-confessed sin or to change us in ways that will be life-giving in the long run but painful in the short term. Will we allow the wind of the Spirit to blow us out of our relatively comfortable—or at least familiar—position and make us start all over as if we were . . . well, being born again?

Choosing this new birth that leads to eternal life might seem like the obvious right choice, but once again human nature can undermine us in a way that leads us to choose destruction over rescue. John 3 brings one more image into the discussion of spiritual transformation: light. "This is the verdict: Light has come into the world, but people loved darkness instead of light because their deeds were evil. Everyone who does evil hates the light, and will not come into the light for fear that their deeds will be exposed" (vv. 19–20). Light is ultimately beautiful and life-giving, but its brightness and clarity can be so stark that we want to hide. Who wants their own sinfulness exposed, even to themselves? Much easier to deny, rationalize, dismiss, or procrastinate dealing with the sin that is in us.

If you step out of a pitch-black room into the brightness of daylight, it can be painful at first. But if you want to *see* anything, such temporary pain is necessary in order to enjoy the benefits that illumination provides. Those who have physical sight know that truth already, so we're willing to move from darkness to light routinely, putting up with the pain until it subsides. The light of the Spirit can be even more painful at first. It strips away our excuses and elaborate defenses that we have used to avoid the knowledge of our own sin. Jesus can wash away the sin and give us life, but it can be tempting to try to stay hidden in the darkness to see if we can avoid confronting the sin altogether. John P. Meier writes that the reason for this "cockroach-like aversion" to the light is that "the evildoer does not want his or her deeds, the building blocks of his or her whole false existence, to be *elengchthē*—a marvelously dense verb that includes the ideas of unmasking, exposing, showing a person up for what he or she is, and hence rebuking, censuring, and convicting."[9]

It takes courage to let the light of the Spirit shine into our lives and expose what is there. It takes faith to believe that the loving God who brings awareness of our sin does so only to rescue us from it. John 3 gives us images to help us grasp this spiritual process. Like Nicodemus, we may struggle to do so. A second birth? Wind of the Spirit? Light and darkness? But if we step forward in faith and let God change us, what can we expect to happen?

What does a person look like who has been born for a second time? Think of what a person looks like who is born for the *first* time. That first birth does not produce a fully formed, independent adult who understands everything and performs flawlessly. Instead, the first birth produces a *baby*, who needs nurture, care, love, patience, teaching, and time to move into his or her full identity. The second birth produces a baby Christian. That baby Christian needs nurture, care, love, patience, teaching, and time to move into her full identity. The baby Christian is still as fully dependent on God as an infant is on his or her parents. But in both cases, the baby has sprung to life. The identity that once did not exist now does. The future is open and new, full of peril in many ways, but also full of ultimate promise.

The Most Famous Verse of All

This entire gospel message of new life is summed up in John 3:16—very briefly, in only twenty-five words in the Greek. That is why people love this verse so much. Theology can get complicated, but the essence of our faith is presented right there so clearly that even a child can understand it. Many of us learned the verse as a child. I memorized it in Sunday school in fourth grade in the King James Version, which is still how it goes through my mind. If someone had asked me at that age to tell them what Christianity was, that verse is what I would have told them. I understood the ideas of God's love, Jesus's sacrifice, and my need to believe. I didn't understand everything about it, of course, and still don't, but I knew enough to know that this was my verse of salvation, of life.

John 3:16 is not part of the conversation between Jesus and Nicodemus, most scholars agree. Instead, it is the Gospel writer's comment reflecting on that conversation. He wrote this sentence after Jesus's death and resurrection in order to bring others to Christ.

Why does this verse carry so much weight? Consider its phrases: **For God so loved the world.** What if he didn't? Many of us are so used to hearing God loves us that it never occurs to us that he could have done anything else. We are his creation, but that doesn't mean he had to love us. I have created plenty of things I don't love. When humanity sinned so outrageously and turned their back on him, God could have wiped out the entire human race and been done with it. Or he could have loved only a few of us and rejected the rest. But God *loved* the world. That is the key to our ultimate rescue. He loves you. Sit back for a moment right now and bask in his love. If you are a person who, like me, spends lots of time running around taking care of responsibilities, meeting deadlines, making things happen, and striving to prevent everything from falling apart, then maybe you have forgotten that, in eternal terms, our future rests not on all this frantic action but on *accepting* God's *love.*

That he gave his one and only Son. God created the universe. He spoke it into being. If the price for rescuing us had been, let's say, fifty or sixty or even a thousand planets, or even that many solar systems, God could have given those without any real cost to himself. What he gave instead was the one thing that *did* cost him—his only Son. The Father, the Son, and the Holy Spirit are the divine members of the Trinity, one God in three Persons in loving relationship for eternity. God's love places a cost on this relationship that is beyond human comprehension. Giving his son meant surrendering him to death on the cross in order to rescue us from the barrier of sin. No one else could have done it. No one else could have given it. Nothing else but his extravagant love for us could have motivated it.

That whoever believes in him shall not perish but have eternal life. The "whoever" means that this gift of eternal life is not restricted by any category. You don't have to be of a certain gender, family background, racial group, ethnic identity, or any other way of dividing people that you can think of. This life is offered to anyone—even you. Receiving this life also does not depend on proving yourself, making yourself worthy, getting your act together, or any other accomplishment you could possibly think of. It only requires that you believe in Christ. Analyzing the Greek term that John uses in this passage, Murray J. Harris shows that this kind of belief is "all-encompassing" and "involves the total commitment of one's whole self to the person of Christ as Messiah and Lord forever."[10] That means relying only on Christ for your rescue and giving up on self-sufficiency. That kind of belief does not mean doubt never arises. It means that even your doubt is something you bring to Christ. You are all in. You have nothing else to rely on but him. You trust him to lead you into a new kind of life that saves you from perishing—from being separated from God—and that is an eternal life that begins not when you die but right now. You are rescued.

John 3 is certainly full of mystery. You can be "born again"? The Spirit is like the wind? Light has come into the world? But in another sense, this chapter is as direct as it can be about God's intent to save you. No wonder these words end up in the most unlikely places, like WWE broadcasts and posters in football stadiums and paper cups in fast food restaurants. People seek hope, and in Jesus Christ they find it. "For God did not send his Son into the world to condemn the world, but to save the world through him" (John 3:17).

Notes

1. "Tim Tebow: John 3:16," *Book Minute* (blog), Museum of the Bible, https://www.museumofthebible.org/book/minutes/359.

2. John Canton, "WWE Has Successfully Trademarked the Term '3:16,'" Uproxx, July 31, 2017, https://uproxx.com/prowrestling/wwe-trademark-316-steve-austin/.

3. Murray J. Harris, *John 3:16: What's It All About?* (Eugene, OR: Cascade Books, 2015), 3.

4. Frederick Dale Bruner, *The Gospel of John: A Commentary* (Grand Rapids: William B. Eerdmans Publishing Company, 2012), 178.

5. Bruner, *Gospel of John*, 178.

6. Bob Smietana, "Two-Thirds of Americans Admit They Are Sinners," *Christianity Today*, August 15, 2017, https://www.christianitytoday.com/news/channel/utilities/print.html?type=article&id=139463.

7. Henri J. M. Nouwen, *The Return of the Prodigal Son: A Story of Homecoming* (New York: Doubleday, 1992), 53.

8. Nouwen, *Return of the Prodigal Son*, 53.

9. John P. Meier, "The Johannine Kerygma: Good News or Bad News?" *Mid-Stream* 41, no. 4, 42.

10. Harris, *John 3:16*, 20.

Digging Deeper

1. John 3:16, or even the 3:16 designation alone, makes many appearances in popular culture, from football games to WWE t-shirts to fast-food restaurant cups. What does that indicate about the significance of this verse? Some uses of the designation are far from its original intent. Should that disturb Christians, or is there another way to look at it?

2. Jesus uses different sets of imagery in John 3 to describe spiritual change. He uses the metaphor of new birth. He talks about the wind of the Spirit blowing through one's life. He speaks of light that shatters the darkness. Review what Jesus says about each of these. How does each one expand your understanding of how God works in people's lives?

3. This chapter discusses a study that shows that a large majority of people believe they are sinners and are not happy about it. However, more people believe they can fix the problem themselves than believe they need to turn to Jesus. Why are people so reluctant to turn to Christ for rebirth?

Go to https://www.thefoundrypublishing.com/12NT/LeaderGuide for a free downloadable leader's guide that includes more questions for reflection as well as activities for use in a small group setting.

7

Jesus Washing Peter's Feet // Ford Madox Brown // c. 1852-1856

Love

²⁸ *One of the teachers of the law came and heard them debating. Noticing that Jesus had given them a good answer, he asked him, "Of all the commandments, which is the most important?"*

²⁹ *"The most important one," answered Jesus, "is this: 'Hear, O Israel: The Lord our God, the Lord is one.* ³⁰ *Love the Lord your God with all your heart and with all your soul and with all your mind and with all your strength.'* ³¹ *The second is this: 'Love your neighbor as yourself.' There is no commandment greater than these."*

—**Mark 12:28–31**

LOVE.

Has any concept in history been more twisted out of shape? Scan through the stations on the radio to hear how love is invoked to describe just about any relationship, from the most casual sexual encounter to the pining away of a lover whose boyfriend has done her wrong. Or turn on the television to see how love is exploited—not only in the shows themselves but also in the advertising.

I am writing at a time when seemingly endless commercials for Subaru pop up on my TV screen, carrying the slogan, "Love. It's what makes a Subaru a Subaru." Really? Love is what makes it a Subaru? Not pistons and gaskets and hoses and tires? The commercials feature sentimental stories of family togetherness with the car in the background, even though viewers learn almost nothing about the car itself. What kind of engine does it have? What's the gas mileage? How much does it cost? You'll never find out from the commercials. But you will be told that this Subaru is an essential component of having love in your life.

Love is used to sell far more than cars, of course. It is exploited to sell just about anything, from blood pressure medication to breakfast cereal to dog food. Advertisers are not alone in using love to promote their agendas. Politicians use it to push their favorite policies, and adulterers use it to rationalize extramarital affairs. Couples fight about it. Poets write about it. Everybody longs for it.

Since love is such an abused idea, it's tempting to steer clear of writing anything about its place in the Bible. Sure, it's there, but it's everywhere else too: the grocery aisles, the department stores, on tattoos, in graffiti, in social media memes, in raunchy videos. Is the concept of love cheapened because corporations tie their automobiles to it, or because a pop musician includes it in a vulgar song? Or do those perversions of it actually show that love is so much at the core of what it means to be human that people can't resist linking things to it, even when those things are gross corruptions of it? Advertisers know you're not going to find authentic love by buying a certain brand of medicine or shampoo or air freshener. But they also know that you have such a deep need for true love that you may be lured—at least long enough for them to get your momentary attention—to anything they connect to even a counterfeit version of love.

You're smart enough to know their tricks, but sometimes you get sucked in anyway, even if you're not fully aware of it. The little boy playing with the puppy during the vacation in the woods with his smiling family—all made possible by that beautiful new automobile in the background—might tug at your heart just enough to make you have positive feelings about that car company the next time you're in the market to buy. That company is all about family love, isn't it? Or, at least, that's what the company hopes you will think. Why would love matter when you're making a car purchase? Because, deep down, you want more than a reliable car. You want love. You yearn for it. You need it. You may need a good car too, but if the company can tap into an even deeper need, you're hooked.

If You Can't Buy Love, Then Where Is It?

If raunchy songs and breakfast cereal offer only a counterfeit love, then where is the real thing? If you had to identify the most loving act that had ever been committed, what would you say? Many Christians, including me, would locate it within what is perhaps the most famous verse of the New Testament, John 3:16: "For God so loved the world that he gave his one and only Son, that whoever believes in him shall not perish but have eternal life." I devote a whole chapter to that passage in this book, but all the other chapters also have love at the core. Love is at the center of the Good Samaritan's actions toward the beaten-up stranger. Love leads the father to embrace his rebellious son in the prodigal son parable. Love radiates through Romans 8 and Acts 2, through the stories of the birth of Jesus, the Last Supper, Jesus's sacrifice on the cross, and certainly his resurrection.

"God is love," says 1 John 4:8. Love defines and motivates God. Love is the driving impulse of the whole Bible, as God reaches out to sinful human beings to draw us to him, love us, forgive us, move us to become more like him, and invite us into eternity with him.

One time a man came up to Jesus and asked, of all the commandments, which one is most important? It was a direct question, and surprisingly, Jesus answered it directly. Why is that surprising? If you've read many of Jesus's answers to questions asked of him, you'll see that he often prefers a more indirect approach, which probably drove some of his questioners crazy. Sometimes the reason for his indirect answer was that the person asking the question wasn't seeking a true answer but was merely trying to trick him. When the chief priests, teachers of the law, and elders asked Jesus by what authority he did what he was doing, for example, Jesus responded not with an answer but with a question. He asked whether they thought John's baptism was of divine or human origin. They were stuck. They had to consult one another to come up with a response. Answer "from heaven," and Jesus would ask why they didn't follow him. Answer the opposite way, and the people who believed John was a prophet might stone them. "We don't know," they said. Jesus responded, "Neither will I tell you by what authority I am doing these things," and that settled that (Luke 20:1–8).

Jesus also answered indirectly when a man asked him what he should do to inherit eternal life, and when someone else asked about paying taxes. So when one of the teachers of the law asks which commandment is most important, I don't really expect Jesus to give a simple answer. *I* certainly wouldn't have wanted to be the one faced with the question of which commandment is the most important of all. I would be tempted to dodge it with something like, "They're *all* important. Follow all of them." Or maybe this would have been a good opportunity for another answer-a-question-with-a-question technique.

Jesus didn't do that. Instead, he gave a response that could not have been more straightforward: "The most important one," answered Jesus, "is this: 'Hear, O Israel: The Lord our God, the Lord is one. Love the Lord your God with all your heart and with all your soul and with all your mind and with all your strength.' The second is this: 'Love your neighbor as yourself.' There is no commandment greater than these" (Mark 12:29-31). With that answer, Jesus put love at the center of the kingdom of God he is ushering in. Love is at the core of Christianity.

Theologian Scot McKnight calls Jesus's answer about the greatest commandment the "Jesus Creed," which is a transformation of the Jewish creed called the *Shema*. The first part of Jesus's answer comes directly from the *Shema* (Deuteronomy 6:4–5). Jesus then adds the second part, which is from Leviticus 19:18. Just as the observant Jew recites the *Shema* each day when waking up and before going to bed, McKnight believes the observant Christian should recite the Jesus Creed each day. He believes Jesus gave it to his followers for their spiritual formation. McKnight repeats it to himself at least once a day, sometimes many more. He says, "It punctuates my morning; it sets a rhythm to my day and settles my day into a comfortable spot. It constantly reminds me, not as a command but as a confession, that whatever I do throughout the day is to be shaped by loving God and loving others."[1]

If the individual Christian wanted to know what to do in order to live more like Christ, nothing could capture it more succinctly than the Jesus Creed. Imagine what would happen to the world if every Christian repeated this call to love every day and did everything in their power to live it out that day.

How Love Has Changed the World

In fact, in many ways too numerous to document, Jesus's emphasis on loving God and loving others *has* changed the world. That is not to say that only Christians know how to love or that only their acts of love are worth noting. Love is a gift of God to all humanity. Love has been diminished by the fall of humanity, but fortunately for all our sakes, the fall did not snuff it out. We see love all around us, and we are allowed to participate in it no matter where we stand with God. But he is its source, and Christ is love's most vivid example.

Turning to Christ means fully knowing love, and being his Christlike follower means fully pursuing love. Christians have practiced love only imperfectly—to put it mildly. Our failures are numerous, as critics are only too happy to point out. In fact, in many instances throughout history, and even today, Christians have done just the opposite of love. Horrible things have been done—and are still being done—by those who claim they do so in Christ's name. Acts of racism, sexism, and institutional corruption of many kinds have been committed by those who call themselves Christians. The church should constantly challenge itself to solidify its commitment to the principle of love that Jesus put at the center of life in his kingdom. Jesus has put the church into the hands of flawed people who are recipients of his love and grace but who are also still being spiritually formed. We will sometimes fail at love, but we are a community who can also lovingly correct one another and put the church back on the right path.

While it is easy—and valid—to criticize the church for its many failures of love, it is also instructive to see the numerous ways in which Christians' commitment to love has made the world a better place. Today, Christians spread love throughout the world in organizations like World Vision, Samaritan's Purse, and the Salvation Army. These organizations love people in tangible ways, such as hurricane relief, medical ministries, clean-water projects, home-building, farming projects, children's projects, educational initiatives, economic empowerment projects, and many other examples. Christian churches all over the world serve the homeless and needy and minister to their communities in endless ways. Many pages could be filled with historical examples of Christians loving those around them. We could look at the history of Christian involvement in the founding of hospitals, inner-city missions, orphanages, and universities. Across the years, millions of people have benefited from these loving acts inspired by Christ's command to love one another.

The world is a less treacherous and less hostile place than it otherwise would be because of the bold initiatives of love from followers of Christ. Some of the love that goes out from Christians is in the form of those big acts, but Scripture also teaches that even the simplest gestures of love are significant. When Jesus was sending out his twelve disciples, he told them, "And if anyone gives even a cup of cold water to one of these little ones who is my disciple, truly I tell you, that person will certainly not lose their reward" (Matthew 10:42).

Love: It's Not So Easy

Love is easy to talk about but harder to practice. One chapter in the Bible that always makes me see how far I fall short of the ideal of love is 1 Corinthians 13, often called the "love chapter." It's one of those passages in Scripture whose familiarity has often obscured rather than deepened people's understanding of it. You hear it quoted out of context at events like weddings, as a poetic little piece of sentimental decoration tacked on to the ceremony like a fringe of icing on the cake.

When I hear a label like the "love chapter," I think "fluff." It evokes images of puppy dogs, hazy sunsets, couples holding hands. Some of the posters I have seen with 1 Corinthians 13 printed on them include a teddy bear holding a big red heart, a silhouette of a man staring out at the ocean, a child holding a flower, a cartoon of a heart-shaped hot-air balloon, a collection of pink roses, and various other images that feature seashores, mountains, toddlers, and serene faces.

The biblical chapter itself, however, is not so sentimental. It is tough. Paul wrote it not because he felt in the mood to write a sappy greeting card but because he was confronting a *problem* in the church. The problem was a prideful spirit that some people had about their spiritual gifts, of all things. Gifts of the Spirit are given to Christians to serve others. Paul lists some of these gifts in chapter 12, such as prophecy, teaching, performing miracles, healing people, and speaking or interpreting tongues. All of these gifts are important, and God has intentionally spread them throughout the church.

The church is like a body, Paul says. A physical body relies on hands, eyes, feet, and other parts. It wouldn't work if the body were made up only of feet. And the ear should not complain because it is not the foot, nor should it feel superior to the foot. Paul is writing to people who have grown prideful about their own gifts to the detriment of others. At the end of the chapter, he says, "And yet I will show you the most excellent way" (12:31b). That way, as Paul goes on to explain in chapter 13, is love. It does no good to have even the most magnificent gifts—the ability to speak in the tongues of men and angels or the faith to move mountains—if we don't have love. Accomplishment of any kind is no replacement for love. What is love? Paul describes it this way: "Love is patient, love is kind. It does not envy, it does not boast, it is not proud. It does not dishonor others, it is not self-seeking, it is not easily angered, it keeps no record of wrongs. Love does not delight in evil but rejoices with the truth. It always protects, always trusts, always hopes, always perseveres" (13:4-7).

What would happen to the world if Christians truly believed and lived out this description of love? What if each of us took one phrase from this and repeated it each day until it really took hold in our lives? *Love keeps no record of wrongs.* How long would it take to learn to stop bringing up that list of failures of a difficult person in your life every time that person confronted you? *Love is patient.* Simple, right? Until your boss or spouse or son or daughter pushes every single button you have and refuses to do the one thing you asked and is *completely* unreasonable even though you have gone the extra mile time and time again.

Love may seem *too* difficult at times, but Paul emphasizes that it is the one thing that will last. All those other gifts you may be tempted to take pride in—like tongues and prophecies—will eventually fade away, but love is eternal. Love is what we should set our hearts on. If that list of the characteristics of love sounds tough to live up to, remember that Paul gave the list as a *contrast* to what he was actually seeing in the church at Corinth. Christians don't always get this right. The same is often true today. Christians can be the most loving people I know, but they can also be the most arrogant and unmerciful people. We don't need to despair over that—we can learn to love better—but we shouldn't be complacent about it either. Paul is calling on Christians to grow up and follow this more excellent way of love.

Being a Christian means being frequently embarrassed by other Christians. Every day on social media and elsewhere, I see a barrage of stories denouncing Christians. These stories—of sex scandals, financial scandals, stupid and hurtful remarks made by Christians, or Christians putting politics ahead of their faith—make me angry and sad. This flood of stories can also make me feel under siege as a Christian because I know they do not tell the whole story. These bad actions are not indicative of the acts of true love and faith that I see from my fellow believers every day. I want to fight back to set the record straight and paint a more balanced picture.

How *should* the church respond to its critics? By blasting them right back in social media posts? Instead, how about overwhelming them with love? What if the followers of Christ showed so much love every day that their reputation became more characterized by love than by anything else? Jesus called on his followers to do that. On the night when Jesus washed his disciples' feet and shared the Last Supper with them, he said, "A new command I give you: Love one another. As I have loved you, so you must love one another. By this everyone will know that you are my disciples, if you love one another" (John 13:34–35). Jesus spoke not just about what they *should* do but about what they would be *known* for doing. They would be *characterized* by love. They would be *stereotyped* by love.

Love Begins Where You Are Right Now

If love is not the stereotype Christians have today, then there is more work to do. As Jesus explained it, love should start with one another. Loving other believers is often harder than loving people we don't know. Get involved with a church for a while and you'll see what I mean. Certain people will annoy you. Some may insult you without realizing it. Others will insult you on purpose. Fellow believers will fail you in any number of ways—they may ignore you, misunderstand you, contradict you, let you down when you need them most, demand too much of you, put you in awkward situations. What are you supposed to do about it? Some simply leave—not only that particular church but the church as a whole. Many have been seriously hurt by the church, and they understandably feel reluctant to open themselves up to further pain by being part of it.

Jesus does not present quitting as an option, though. He presents love as *the* option. On that final night when Jesus commanded his disciples to love one another, he knew that betrayal by one of his disciples, Judas Iscariot, was already in motion. That very betrayal would lead to Jesus's crucifixion. Jesus also knew that Peter would soon deny him before the rooster crowed, and he knew the rest of them would scatter once he was arrested. Still, he washed their feet. He loved them. These men were his closest friends and should have been the people he knew he could count on the most. But, like the church today, the disciples were flawed people in need of saving.

After his resurrection, Jesus sent the disciples out to the entire world, telling them, "Therefore go and make disciples of all nations, baptizing them in the name of the Father and of the Son and of the Holy Spirit, and teaching them to obey everything I have commanded you" (Matthew 28:19–20). That was a huge task, but loving the whole world never starts with "the whole world." Jesus first had to teach them to love one another. That's where he starts with us too.

How do we do it? Jesus gave examples. When he described to his disciples how his true followers would be ushered into his kingdom in eternity, he said he would welcome them with the words, "For I was hungry and you gave me something to eat, I was thirsty and you gave me something to drink, I was a stranger and you invited me in, I needed clothes and you clothed me, I was sick and you looked after me, I was in prison and you came to visit me" (Matthew 25:35–36). They will ask him when they ever did such things for him, and his response will be, "Truly I tell you, whatever you did for one of the least of these brothers and sisters of mine, you did for me" (v. 40). Love may start with the simple act of giving a thirsty person something to drink. Eventually you may be called to undertake even greater achievements that will feed thousands or overturn unjust systems, but the fact that you or the church can't fix everything does not give you an excuse for doing nothing. Love one another, Jesus commands. Start where you are.

The local church of which I am a member is one that, from the outside, would be easy for critics to stereotype as insular and out of touch with the painful realities beyond our walls. It's a suburban, mostly white, mostly middle-class congregation. However, a closer look shows many ways in which this congregation is showing Christ's love every day. Our church has prepared hundreds of crisis care kits for victims of hurricanes and other disasters. Some of our members have walked to raise funds for diabetes research; others have trained on behalf of World Vision for the Los Angeles Marathon to raise money for clean-water projects in Africa. Each month our church members work for a ministry called More than a Meal, making and serving sack lunches to those in need. A church member hosted a yard sale to raise money for a mission trip to Nepal. We also have an ongoing relationship with a church in Belize, where our members have helped build a school. We have built homes in Mexico and sponsored mission trips for teens and adults to many places in the United States and around the world. We serve a foster care program run by Los Angeles County. The list could go on, and these are only some of the ways that our church members reach out to people *outside* the church.

There are also vibrant ministries *within* the church. Small groups and Sunday school classes meet to pray with one another about the most pressing issues of their lives. I have taught one such group for more than ten years, and we have become good friends who help each other out, listen to one another, celebrate with each other, and grieve with one another. The acts of love in that class alone could fill a chapter—rides to doctor appointments, gifts and loans to needy people, supportive phone calls made at just the right time, and deep discussions of the Bible and the challenges of living the Christian life.

Someone close to me fell out of love with the church because he felt it didn't fully embrace him, even though he had been attending for a long time. He felt like a stranger, so it was easy to simply drift away. How could that have been prevented? To me, it looked as if people *did* embrace him, but even if his perception was correct, then my suggestion would have been to solidify his relationships with his fellow church members by serving. Find a way to help out.

I don't know of any church that is not eager for help to carry out its mission. Churches need ushers and greeters. They need workers for the children's programs, people to chaperone youth trips and events, people to run sound for worship services, volunteers to prepare meals for funeral dinners, people willing to give rides to older congregants who can no longer drive, participants to go on mission trips, skilled workers to do repairs to the church building, volunteers to make coffee for social times between services, and a thousand other tasks. The people I know who feel most connected at church are the ones who spend time serving. If your church has not embraced you fully enough, maybe your response should be to jump in and be the one who does the embracing.

You Can Afford to Be Generous

One of the most fulfilling realities of life is when you *know* someone loves you. Think for a moment about the one or two people in your life who love you the most, who treasure you, and whom you could count on no matter what. In John 15:9, Jesus says to his disciples, "As the Father has loved me, so have I loved you. Now remain in my love." Scripture tells us repeatedly that God loves us, but I often still have trouble grasping it deep inside me. The love of God often feels like love God is *required* to have. Sure, he loves everybody, but—I don't *feel* that, deep in my bones.

When I know someone loves me, I see my life differently as a result. I'm more joyful, more secure, and my life has more purpose because I have that person to share things with and someone who *cares* about what is happening to me. I want to know God's love as more than a mere concept. If I have not absorbed his love into the essence of who I am, then it is harder to muster the spiritual generosity and confidence to reach out to others in love.

As I was preparing to teach a lesson recently that had to do with God's love, I realized that, even though I am a Christian, it had been a while since I had thought of God's love in the way that I think of the love of other people in my life. God's love was an abstraction. I decided to spend time each day sitting still and knowing that God loved me. As I sat there for ten or fifteen minutes a day, I repeated the words, "I am a beloved child of God." I read scriptures, mostly from Romans 8, that talked about God's love. I read about those who are led by the Spirit being the children of God. I read about being adopted by God, and calling him Abba Father, and his Spirit testifying with my spirit that I am God's child. What if this is really true? *I am a beloved child of God.* What does that mean? What does it mean that I love *my* children? It means I have their ultimate good in mind. I would do anything for them. I have been championing them even before they were born, and ever since.

For days I contemplated God's love and nothing else during these sessions. It felt a little awkward at first. After a few days, it felt more natural. God loves *me*. God *loves* me. *God* loves me. What difference will it make when I get up from here and go about my life? At one point a sentence came to me that kept running through my mind for days: *You can afford to be generous.* Without realizing it, I had been approaching life as a game in which resources were so tight and God's provision so limited that I had to put all my energy into securing things: opportunities, my family's well-being, my reputation, and the list went on. Life felt like a competition in which I was constantly trying to grab some prize that someone else might steal out of my hands if I didn't guard it carefully.

What if I discarded the competition metaphor? What if I instead saw myself as a child of God whom God really loves? I know he loves me, and even if I don't always understand how and where he is leading me, I so believe in that love that I can *rest* in it even in the worst circumstances. He has other children—my brothers and sisters—and he wants me to love them freely just as he loves me because there is plenty of love to go around. *You can afford to be generous.* I can afford to focus on how something affects someone else more than I need to focus on how it affects me. I don't have to worry that someone else has more than me, is outdoing me—because *I am loved.* There is plenty to go around. I can afford to be generous. I can afford to love.

Notes

1. Scot McKnight, *The Jesus Creed* (Brewster, MA: Paraclete Press, 2004), 12.

Digging Deeper

1. Love is exploited by advertisers, songwriters, politicians, and celebrities. Does that exploitation make it harder to understand love in the ways that Jesus spoke about it? Does our popular culture's constant focus on love show how deeply people long for authentic love? How can you tell the difference between what is real and what is counterfeit?

2. This chapter points out that Jesus wanted Christians to be known for love, but they often have failed miserably at this. What examples can you think of when Christians have failed at love? On the other hand, Christians are also known for selfless acts of love, both large and small. What examples come to mind? Does the church do enough to put love at the core of its mission?

3. Christians often face criticism and feel under siege by those who don't approve of us. The chapter suggests that, rather than fighting back with snarky social media posts or defensive rebuttals, Christians should overwhelm their critics with love. What are some ways that could be done?

4. We often hear that God loves us, but as the author points out, it is sometimes hard to think about that love as more than an abstraction. What can you do that would help you *know* that God loves you?

Go to https://www.thefoundrypublishing.com/12NT/LeaderGuide for a free downloadable leader's guide that includes more questions for reflection as well as activities for use in a small group setting.

Jesus's Followers in Motion

8

Pentecost // El Greco // c. 1541-1614

Acts 2

¹ When the day of Pentecost came, they were all together in one place. ² Suddenly a sound like the blowing of a violent wind came from heaven and filled the whole house where they were sitting. ³ They saw what seemed to be tongues of fire that separated and came to rest on each of them. ⁴ All of them were filled with the Holy Spirit and began to speak in other tongues as the Spirit enabled them.

³⁸ Peter replied, "Repent and be baptized, every one of you, in the name of Jesus Christ for the forgiveness of your sins. And you will receive the gift of the Holy Spirit. ³⁹ The promise is for you and your children and for all who are far off—for all whom the Lord our God will call."

⁴⁰ With many other words he warned them; and he pleaded with them, "Save yourselves from this corrupt generation." ⁴¹ Those who accepted his message were baptized, and about three thousand were added to their number that day.

⁴² They devoted themselves to the apostles' teaching and to fellowship, to the breaking of bread and to prayer. ⁴³ Everyone was filled with awe at the many wonders and signs performed by the apostles. ⁴⁴ All the believers were together and had everything in common. ⁴⁵ They sold property and possessions to give to anyone who had need. ⁴⁶ Every day they continued to meet together in the temple courts. They broke bread in their homes and ate together with glad and sincere hearts, ⁴⁷ praising God and enjoying the favor of all the people. And the Lord added to their number daily those who were being saved.

—Acts 2:1–4, 38–47

LIKE JOHN 3:16 or Romans 8:28, Acts 2 is one of those passages of the Bible so famous that people recognize it by its chapter reference alone. When I was a teenager, one of the most popular Christian music groups was called the Second Chapter of Acts. Many other Christian organizations and programs now link their causes to that chapter. The 2:47 Network, which draws its name from that verse in Acts, partners with congregations and Christian leaders to plant churches. The Acts 2 Journey Initiative is a ministry in which a group of consultants helps churches to become more alive and effective. The Acts 2 Church in Virginia Beach, Virginia, is dedicated to helping people become fully committed followers of Christ. A church in Falls River, Wisconsin, is named The Acts 2 Fellowship Church, and one in Edmond, Oklahoma, is called Acts 2 United Methodist Church. And the list goes on.

As with other famous passages of the Bible, plenty of products have been created to celebrate Acts 2, including decals, signs, and license plate covers. Many of those items feature the portion of verses 46-47 that says, "They broke bread in their homes and ate together with glad and sincere hearts, praising God and enjoying the favor of all the people."

The reason this chapter of the Bible is so important is that it tells of the birth of the church. It describes the outpouring of the Holy Spirit that brought dramatic growth to the Christian movement—not only in that small geographic area to which it was then confined but, ultimately, to every part of the globe. There were 3,000 new converts to Christianity that day. That's an impressive rate of growth, considering there were only about 120 followers of Christ up to that point.

But that was only the beginning. In Acts 1, Jesus had promised even more before his ascension. He told the disciples that what was about to happen would make them his witnesses to the "ends of the earth." Could any of the people present on that day of Pentecost have imagined what that prediction would really mean for the world?

Two thousand years later, how well has what began on that dramatic day prospered? Today, there are more than 2 billion Christians across the world. Let that sink in for a moment. The population of the entire world in Jesus's day was about 300 million. Only 120 of those were followers of Christ at the beginning of the day of Pentecost. But now, the number of followers of Christ is about seven times the population of the entire world at that time. Christianity is now represented by about 35,000 denominations and around 3.5 million local churches. There are more than a million full-time clergy, more than 5 million full-time Christian workers, and about half a million full-time missionaries.[1] The fire that hovered on the day of Pentecost continues to burn brightly throughout the world.

The church is more than just numbers, of course. When the Holy Spirit released his power on the church, and the "sound like the blowing of a violent wind came from heaven" and filled the room as tongues of fire came to rest on the believers' heads, it was not a one-time historical event that was over within an hour or two. That wind of the Spirit kept blowing and still blows today. The wind of the Spirit has blown through the world in ways that are easy to recognize and in ways that are often overlooked.

One obvious manifestation of the Spirit is that the message of Jesus Christ—his death, resurrection, and eternal rescue of those who follow him—has penetrated every corner of the world. But the wind of the Spirit has blown through the world in countless other ways as well. How many songs has the Spirit inspired? How many paintings and sculptures bear the Spirit's influence? How many poems contain within them hints of the Spirit's voice? How many books, how many acts of kindness, how many hospitals, teen camps, care packages, visits to shut-ins, inspired moments, weddings, funerals, evenings with friends, walks through the woods, and countless other details bear the mark of the Holy Spirit? Not every manifestation of the Spirit is as dramatic as on the day of Pentecost. In fact, few are. But, just as the gospel has spread to every corner of the world, so has the Holy Spirit reached in to every aspect of life. The Spirit's presence is often ignored or misunderstood, just as it was brushed off by so many on that awe-inspiring Pentecost day.

Something Big Was about to Happen

Jesus's first followers may not have been able to imagine the billions of fellow believers and millions of churches that would be spawned by the event they were witnessing, but leading up to that historic day, they did have some warning that something big was about to happen. I would give anything to have been part of the events described in Acts 2, but what happens in Acts 1 is pretty remarkable too. Like so many passages in the Bible, it gives tantalizing hints of events for which my imagination would love to fill in the details.

Over a period of forty days after Jesus's resurrection, we are told, he appeared to his disciples, even sat and ate with them, and talked about the kingdom of God. I wish I could have sat in on even a few minutes of these talks! What must Jesus have said? What did the disciples ask him? What were they worried about? How confident were they about the future?

Jesus told them to stay in Jerusalem because they were about to be baptized with the Holy Spirit. They would receive power when the Holy Spirit came upon them, and they would be Christ's "witnesses in Jerusalem, and in all Judea and Samaria, and to the ends of the earth" (1:8). Those were the last words he spoke to them before he ascended into heaven, leaving them dumbfounded, no doubt wondering what it all meant. What would it mean to be baptized with the Holy Spirit? What would this power look like? What would it mean to be his witnesses to the ends of the earth? How could they possibly get the message out so far? Their movement was confined to a small geographical area, and their numbers were modest. The world is a big place—how was this message-spreading supposed to work, exactly? They weren't given answers. They had to wait.

Only one of the disciples' specific questions about their upcoming baptism of the Holy Spirit is recorded in Scripture, and even that question isn't fully answered. They asked, "Lord, are you at this time going to restore the kingdom to Israel?" (1:6). Good question! Where was all of this headed? What was the plan? Jesus says, "It is not for you to know the times or dates the Father has set by his own authority" (v. 7). Any Christian who has prayed for answers to details about the future—or even about the present—will recognize this kind of answer from God. The Holy Spirit plants a calling or sense of direction deep within us, but the Spirit doesn't lay out every step it will take to get there. We have to move forward and trust God.

When Jesus talked about his followers being his witnesses to the ends of the earth, it might sound like hype. In our day of nonstop advertising and sensational claims, we have learned to take such statements with a grain of salt. But Jesus wasn't exaggerating. His gospel really would be taken to the entire world—even parts of it his disciples didn't know existed. And Jesus wasn't simply *asking* them to become his witnesses, or commanding it, or giving them a pep talk. He was *declaring* that it *would* happen.

But really, who were they to carry out such a huge undertaking? If you have read Matthew, Mark, Luke, or John, you will know that, although the disciples certainly had their moments of strong faith and courage, they were also prone to misunderstanding, fear, and betrayal. Is this who Jesus wanted to lead the most significant movement in the history of the world?

They couldn't do it on their own. Not even close. Even the most talented, educated, dynamic, and entrepreneurial group that could have been assembled—which they were not—would not have been able to fulfill the mission Jesus was announcing. That's why the Holy Spirit had to come. As biblical commentator Paul L. Maier points out, "Jesus repeatedly foresaw the problem of a message too powerful for the messengers," so that's why he promised, during the Last Supper, to send the Holy Spirit to help them.[2]

The Fire of the Spirit Descends

To their credit, these followers of Jesus did stay in Jerusalem and wait, as Jesus told them to do, and when the Holy Spirit came, they were ready. It's interesting to consider the different ways the Holy Spirit might have chosen to manifest on that crucial day. He might have shaken the whole city with an earthquake. He might have filled the air with music or a dazzling light show. Think of all the ostentatious special effects a Hollywood moviemaker might use for such a scene. This could have been followed by an array of superpowers given to those in attendance—the ability to walk through walls, or heal people with a single touch, or fly through the air, or many other possibilities.

Certainly the event itself was dramatic enough—the sound of a violent wind blowing through the room and tongues of fire settling on everyone's heads—but this was not about creating a spectacle or turning the gospel into a science-fiction movie. If the baptism of the Holy Spirit was only about showing God's power or giving godlike powers to humans, then God could easily have arranged a display far more flamboyant than what happened at Pentecost. He created the universe. Spectacle was easy.

God wasn't showing off that day. He was building the church. What was the first action the people in that room took when the fire of the Holy Spirit settled on them? They "began to speak in other tongues as the Spirit enabled them" (2:4). Why that power, of all the ones God could have conferred? As verse 5 says, "Now there were staying in Jerusalem God-fearing Jews from every nation under heaven." The timing of the coming of the Holy Spirit was not random. Thousands of pilgrims speaking a variety of languages had come to Jerusalem to celebrate *Shavuot*, or the Festival of Weeks, one of the most important events in the Jewish calendar. Many Christians now associate the word "Pentecost" only with the events of that great day in Christian history, but the word actually derives from the Greek word for "fifty." The feast was to take place about seven weeks, or fifty days, from Passover.

When the people from all these faraway places heard the sound of this violent wind from heaven, they came running. A crowd gathered. To the amazement of these outsiders, they heard "the wonders of God" being proclaimed in their own languages. They stayed around for Peter's sermon. He preached the gospel message of Jesus Christ and urged them to repent and be baptized. More than three thousand new believers came to Christ that day. That number of converts would be significant even if all of them were local Jerusalem residents, but many of these new followers of Christ now would take the gospel message back home with them. The spread of the Christian message to far-off places, as Jesus had promised, had begun on the first day of the Holy Spirit's coming. Rather than sending messengers to the nations, God had begun by sending the nations to the messengers. The miracle of languages propelled the church forward.

The brilliance of what happened on the day of Pentecost is not that it was a one-time miracle to end all miracles designed to dazzle the world, or some

Hollywood production designed to make people "ooh!" and "ah!" An event like that would have quickly faded. The miracle of Pentecost was a dramatic but limited show of God's power to get the process of the spread of the gospel started—a process that continues to this day, of believers telling others and taking it around the world. Miracles still happen, but spectacle is not how the message of Jesus Christ is spread on a day-to-day basis. Instead, the process happens more quietly and humbly, through the work of churches, relationships, faith, worship, preaching, teaching, and trust in God.

Or Were They Just Drunk?

The coming of the Holy Spirit on the day of Pentecost is one of the greatest moments in church history, but it didn't take long before a sour note was introduced into the story. At the high point of the story, when the building was full of the Holy Spirit, when people from all around came running to find out what the roaring wind was, when tongues of fire filled the room and people throughout the building miraculously spoke the languages of nations all over the world, the writer pauses for verse 13, which lands with a thud: "Some, however, made fun of them and said, 'They have had too much wine.'"

Although the event these people witnessed was so amazing that it should have left them awestruck, for some it aroused only mockery. The same thing happens in the world today. Mockery and sarcasm dominate the tone of discussion in our culture today. Scroll through your favorite social media sites and see how often people mock those with different views from their own. Listen to the mockery of comedians. Hear the sarcasm in the voices of the guests on television news shows. We're inundated with people making fun of just about everything—literally nothing is sacred.

Peter denied the charge that the people were drunk, but he didn't seem surprised by it. By now he and the other followers of Christ were used to derision. Jesus himself had endured humiliating mockery just weeks before, leading up to his execution. Luke 22 reports that, after Jesus's arrest, "the men who were guarding Jesus began mocking and beating him. They blindfolded him and demanded, 'Prophesy! Who hit you?' And they said many other insulting things to him" (vv. 63–64).

Those who have experienced the intense joy of a time when the Holy Spirit's presence is particularly close know that it is so overwhelming that it's possible the people *did* appear drunk. The Spirit is intoxicating. One of the aspects of Christianity that those who are not in the faith have trouble understanding is that our relationship with Christ is fueled not only by doctrine and ideas but also by the presence of the Holy Spirit. The Spirit's presence can bring joy that makes people want to sing and dance and cry and shout. He sometimes shows up dramatically and sometimes quietly. He sometimes confronts us directly and other times with the merest hints.

I have been in worship services in which the Spirit's presence is so palpable that it almost feels as if he is physically in the room. These times can be incredibly emotional. I have also experienced the Holy Spirit's guidance in ways that are far less emotional but just as clear in the sense that I must do a certain thing or refrain from doing something. I must speak up or stay silent or call someone or say no to an opportunity or say yes to a request. He can bring peace that passes understanding even in the worst circumstances. He can bring the conviction of knowing that something in my life is sinful and that I need to repent and ask forgiveness for it.

That's what the presence of the Holy Spirit means to a Christian, but how to explain this? It's so easy to dismiss it, to ridicule it, just as the naysayers did on that astonishing day of Pentecost. People scoff at things that don't fit their worldview. I might mock the Holy Spirit myself if I had not experienced his presence so many times so powerfully. Even as a child, I sensed his presence as he drew me toward him and toward the need to turn to faith in Jesus Christ. I know people have ways to try to explain away the experiences Christians have had with the Holy Spirit, but throughout my life I have not been able to escape my conviction that his presence is real. I have staked my life on it, as have millions of other believers.

If not for the animating presence of the Holy Spirit, I believe Christianity would not have survived even a few years. The religious establishment was hostile to it, as were political authorities. But the Holy Spirit's presence has given people the courage to keep following Christ through persecution, hardship, danger, isolation, and misunderstanding. Because of the Holy Spirit, the church has even overcome its own failures, surviving scandal, financial woes, power struggles, immaturity, and every other kind of transgression that should have sunk the whole thing. The church has had to repent, ask forgiveness, and change its ways in order to get back on track. Today some still predict the demise of Christianity, but I am confident it will survive every onslaught, just as Jesus said when he promised Peter that the gates of hell would not prevail against it.

Peter Can't Wait to Get Started

By the time the Holy Spirit enveloped them on the day of Pentecost, Peter and the other disciples had endured far too much resistance to let some scoffers deter them. Peter stood to address the crowd. He was ready to preach the gospel right away. The time of waiting was over. The church was in motion. He dismissed the accusation of drunkenness quickly and got right to his message. What happened on that day was a fulfillment of prophecy, and Peter connected Jesus to the Scripture his audience revered. Then, as would happen countless millions of times in the years and centuries to come, he invited them to follow Christ: "Repent and be baptized, every one of you, in the name of Jesus Christ for the forgiveness of your sins. And you will receive the gift of the Holy Spirit" (Acts 2:38).

With three thousand new believers baptized in a single day, and some of them no doubt headed to their far-off homes to tell about Jesus in their own languages, Acts 2 next gives us a glimpse of how the church functioned on a day-to-day basis. "They devoted themselves to the apostles' teaching and to fellowship, to the breaking of bread and to prayer" (v. 42). Those are some of the essentials that churches still practice today—gathering for worship, caring for one another's needs, praying, breaking bread.

However, a church that would expand to include millions of individual congregations across all the continents in many cultures would need flexibility on how it operates. The church is constantly changing. Thirty or forty years is a mere blip in church history, but I have seen big changes in that amount of time in how the church conducts itself, even within my own limited cultural context. The formality of dress, the style of sermons, the use of technology, the choice of songs and music styles, and many other changes have been made rapidly.

My context is an American Protestant church, and neither the customs we follow now nor the ones we followed thirty years ago would work for a church today in China or Brazil or Africa. And if you take any Christian church anywhere in the world from three hundred years ago or nine hundred years ago, much of what we do in my church today would not even have been technologically possible, nor would it have made much sense to those congregations even if it were possible. But all congregations, throughout the history of the church, can relate to and adapt the simple description of the ways the early church gathered together and worked out the loving mandates of following Christ.

The rest of Acts shows that the unleashing of the power of the Holy Spirit that happened on the day of Pentecost continued dramatically in the days and years that followed. People like Paul turned from hostility to passionate and courageous advocacy of Christianity. He and others journeyed far from home to establish and encourage Christian churches as widely as the limited modes of travel in that day would allow. The news was not all good. Bickering, sin, and misunderstanding from within the church sometimes hampered the Spirit's work, and persecution from powerful people cost the lives of some Christians and led to the imprisonment of others. Even in the midst of persecution, and sometimes because of it, the gospel spread. When Paul was in prison, he did not waste time bemoaning his fate. Instead, he spread the gospel message to anyone who would listen, and he wrote letters that became the bulk of the New Testament.

Just as the Christian journey was not always easy for early Christian leaders like Paul and Peter, everyday Christians of that era also struggled to live out their faith. Acts 2 shows the church at its best, but much of the rest of the New Testament focuses on problems the various congregations had as they worked out what it meant to be followers of Christ. Sometimes they made a mess of things, but their failures did not destroy the church. The church continued through the centuries, with more failures mixed in with the life-changing Christian message. Human failure should have crushed it, but the Holy Spirit never gave up.

Today, the church across the world is beautifully diverse, encompassing people of nearly every nationality, race, and cultural tradition. Some worship in t-shirts and shorts, sipping coffee in paper cups as they sing worship songs projected on a screen. Some wear suits and dresses and follow a carefully prescribed liturgy presented in towering cathedrals. Some join together in shacks with dirt floors. Some meet in secret, knowing at any moment that the hymn they are singing could be their last, with imprisonment or death as likely for them as Sunday dinner is for Christians in more tolerant nations. Even churches whose members don't face imminent physical danger still face perils of many different kinds—apathy, bad theology, insularity. Still, the message of Jesus Christ moves forward through these imperfect institutions.

For churches of every kind, Acts 2 is a message of hope and challenge of what could be. It shows that Jesus's disciples—who once deserted him or denied him or cowered in rooms wondering what would happen next—could be empowered by the Holy Spirit to act courageously beyond what they could have done in their own human strength. The church was set loose on the world, never to be destroyed.

When I stand worshiping in my own church, singing praise to God as the Holy Spirit sweeps through the room, I am tied to that event at Pentecost. The wind that roared through that room with Peter and the other believers that morning never died out. It still blows through my church in California today, and all across the world. We may not always hear that wind or feel it as strongly as they did, but it still swirls, inviting us into its flow.

Notes

1. David Barrett and Todd Johnson, "Global Diagram 24," *World Christian Trends: AD 30–AD 2200: Interpreting the Annual Christian Megacensus* (Pasadena: William Carey Library, 2001), http://www.gordonconwell.edu/ockenga/research/documents/gd24.pdf.

2. Paul L. Maier, *First Christians: Pentecost and the Spread of Christianity* (New York: Harper & Row, 1976), 12.

Digging Deeper

1. This chapter discusses the supernatural ways the Holy Spirit worked on the day of Pentecost and the ways the Spirit is still working today. Scoffers questioned whether the Christians were drunk that day, and critics of Christianity today continue to mock its supernatural elements. What evidence do you see—big or small—of the Holy Spirit's continued presence in people's lives? In what ways do people still dismiss the Holy Spirit's influence?

2. Imagine what it must have been like to be part of the small group of Christians in the days leading up to Pentecost. If you had been among them, what do you think you would have been worried about? Confused about? Hopeful about?

3. Make a list of major obstacles Christianity has faced over the past two thousand years that might have destroyed it if the Holy Spirit had not been present. When you consider that list, what does it make you think about the current challenges to the survival of the Christian faith?

Go to https://www.thefoundrypublishing.com/12NT/LeaderGuide for a free downloadable leader's guide that includes more questions for reflection as well as activities for use in a small group setting.

9

Christ in the Garden of Olives // Eugene Delacroix // 1824

Romans 8

¹⁶ *The Spirit himself testifies with our spirit that we are God's children.*

¹⁸ *I consider that our present sufferings are not worth comparing with the glory that will be revealed in us.*

²² *We know that the whole creation has been groaning as in the pains of childbirth right up to the present time.*

²⁶ *In the same way, the Spirit helps us in our weakness. We do not know what we ought to pray for, but the Spirit himself intercedes for us through wordless groans.*

²⁸ *And we know that in all things God works for the good of those who love him, who have been called according to his purpose.*

³¹ *If God is for us, who can be against us?*

³⁷ *No, in all these things we are more than conquerors through him who loved us.* ³⁸ *For I am convinced that neither death nor life, neither angels nor demons, neither the present nor the future, nor any powers,* ³⁹ *neither height nor depth, nor anything else in all creation, will be able to separate us from the love of God that is in Christ Jesus our Lord.*
—*Romans 8:16, 18, 22, 26, 28, 31b, 37–39*

THE BIBLE CONTAINS many eloquent and memorable passages, but for beauty of language and significance of meaning, few if any chapters soar like Romans 8. In my own Bible reading, this is a chapter I can easily get stuck on. I want to read it repeatedly, like a favorite song I never get tired of no matter how many times it plays. In fact, to me this chapter feels as if it should somehow be set to music, or at least accompanied by it, in order to capture its emotional sweep. Some biblical passages cry out to be painted, the way Rembrandt captured the prodigal son. Other passages call out to be reenacted, the way we recreate the Last Supper with Communion or put on Christmas plays to celebrate Christ's birth. But Romans 8 needs something different—its own "Hallelujah Chorus" treatment or some other musical accompaniment that could do justice to its sweeping words. Ordinary speech is not enough. This chapter vibrates with life.

Christian leaders across the centuries have heaped praise on Romans 8. Popular Christian author Mark Batterson wrote a whole book on it called *If*. In it he tells of other influential Christians who have appreciated it. Martin Luther labeled it "the clearest gospel of them all," William Tyndale said it was "the most excellent part of the New Testament," and John Piper says it is the greatest chapter in the Bible.[1]

Probably the most famous verse in the chapter is verse 28, which has become like John 3:16 to some extent—so famous that many know it by the chapter and verse reference even without hearing the words. One company sells a charm necklace that simply says "R 8:28." And, of course, almost every imaginable kind of product can be purchased with the actual words of the verse on them: mouse pads, coasters, posters, notebooks, bracelets, blankets, luggage tags, flasks, cups, cake toppers, puzzles, picture frames, mugs, buttons, dog tags, wrapping paper, tote bags, notecards, serving trays, and just about any other object on which it is possible to print something.

Romans 8:28 is deeply implanted within the Christian mindset. A Google search yielded 71,000 videos alone dedicated to that verse. There are sermons on it, songs about it, readings of it, stories that illustrate its teaching, and more. We will take a more careful look at why this verse is so popular and also how it has sometimes been abused, but it's important to realize that Romans 8:28 is only one of several verses in that chapter that Christians love to embrace as crucial to their faith. If Romans 8 were an album, 8:28 might be the number-one hit single, but this blockbuster album would have other hits too.

The Symphony of Romans 8

Why is Romans 8 so influential and beloved? The chapter reveals the possibility of a closeness to God that is at the center of the Christian faith. It articulates the core of what we long for as Christians: "the Spirit you received brought about your adoption to sonship. And by him we cry, 'Abba, Father'" (v. 15). Romans 8 emphasizes the totality of the solution that Christ is. He is the ultimate answer to the separation of human beings from God, and he is the beginning of the reversal of the corruption of God's creation. As part of Eugene Peterson's translation of verses 3–4 states it in The Message, "God went for the jugular when he sent his own Son. He didn't deal with the problem as something remote and unimportant. In his Son, Jesus, he personally took on the human condition, entered the disordered mess of struggling humanity in order to set it right once and for all."

Many outsiders to Christianity miss that liberating message. They think of the Christian faith as mainly a set of beliefs and rules to which its followers adhere, but Christ followers know that, while those beliefs are crucial, what brought many of us into the faith—and what keeps many of us in it in spite of suffering and doubt and assault of every kind—is an actual *relationship* with

God that holds us tight and will not let us go. "The Spirit himself testifies with our spirit that we are God's children" (v. 16).

The Christian faith is also forward-looking. We take eternity seriously. And if you take eternity seriously, then you know that the eternity that stretches out in front of us is far longer and more significant than the present reality we are experiencing. But the present reality often *feels* long and difficult. Its demands and its pain can lead us to perceive the present as more *real* than what comes later. We long for the next phase, but we feel tied up in this phase too. The world as it is now, shattered and suffering, is not the way it was designed to be, despite the hints of God's love that suffuse it. Those hints only increase our longing for what's next. "We know that the whole creation has been groaning as in the pains of childbirth right up to the present time" (v. 22). We're groaning too! But in the meantime, we hang on.

What gives us the confidence to keep going? The Holy Spirit Paul describes is a God of action. He lives and breathes in us and brings us life. He rescues us from a life of sin. He beckons us toward a life of expectancy, facing life's challenges head on in the confident knowledge that he is powerfully, unwaveringly *on our side. He is for us.* The joy of eternity is going to be so overwhelming that it will make our current suffering look tiny by comparison—so says Paul, who suffered extensively throughout his life.

Sometimes we get so discouraged we feel too spiritually weak even to cry out to God. But the Holy Spirit helps us even with that. "We do not know what we ought to pray for, but the Spirit himself intercedes for us through wordless groans" (v. 26). Look at our situation. Jesus died for us and was raised to life for us and is now in the Father's presence advocating for us. Nothing can cut off that love or that connection we now have to Christ. No matter what anyone does to us, or how unfair or tragic our circumstances are, or how much pain we feel, or how many powers are aligned against us, the ultimate truth is that God's love will bring us through to a glorious eternity. "No, in all these things we are more than conquerors through him who loved us" (v. 37).

Stop and Read It

That is a quick overview of some of the big ideas in Romans 8, but a summary is not enough. Someone could ask you to summarize your favorite song, but would a summary alone communicate its beauty? Only *hearing* the song allows you to fully experience it. Romans 8 is similar. Even if its famous lines are so familiar to you that you think you know it, there is no substitute to experiencing all of it together. That's why I am going to do something I never do in any of my books, and that is to suggest that, if you have not read all of Romans 8 recently, you put down this book and pick up that chapter. Start near the end of Romans 7 and continue through the entirety of chapter 8, letting the words wash over you. If you are so inclined, read it in more than one version, perhaps The Message and the New International Version and one or two others. There are plenty of theological fine points to analyze verse by verse, and we will do that in the pages to come, but first, don't let yourself miss out on the joyful music of the chapter.

How thrilling it is when you can see this chapter afresh. How meaningful to read it in a mindset in which you know in the depths of your soul that its message is true. "If God is for us, then who can be against us?" (v. 31b). What could we not withstand if we truly believed that? What if we lived as if we had no doubt about those words? For most of us, the words of this chapter get diluted. We doubt. We *want* to believe but sometimes wonder if it's merely happy talk, hyperbole, if there's somehow a catch. Romans 8 connects with every aspect of how we connect with God: our intellect, our emotions, our intuition, our imagination. Let the words sink deep into your soul.

Romans 8—The Meaning beyond the Greatest Hits

Romans 8 is more than a list of inspiring sayings to slap on a poster or to decorate a coffee mug. It may resemble a greatest-hits album, but it also sets forth the essence of the gospel: Christ sets us free. We don't have to try to save ourselves. Christ entered the otherwise hopeless realm of bound-up and doomed humanity and unchained us. We are liberated—if only we accept the liberation.

Romans 8:1–4

These four verses encapsulate the Christian message. Chapter 7 has raised the dilemma of sin in which all of us are caught, and it has shown the inadequacy of the law to address it. Paul describes the dilemma this way: "Although I want to do good, evil is right there with me. For in my inner being I delight in God's law; but I see another law at work in me, waging war against the law of my mind and making me a prisoner of the law of sin at work within me. What a wretched man I am! Who will rescue me from this body that is subject to death?" (7:21b–24).

Jesus Christ is the rescuer. As Peterson translates Romans 8:1 in the Message, "With the arrival of Jesus, the Messiah, that fateful dilemma is resolved." The problem of sin was deep and entrenched within humanity. The solution had to be extreme. James D. G. Dunn explains, "The cancer of sin had taken such a firm root on the flesh, on humankind, that the surgery had to be radical; the flesh had to be destroyed, humankind had to die. The old age had to be wound up and a new beginning made." Christ brought that new beginning. His "complete oneness with sinful flesh meant that his death effected the destruction of that sinful flesh, just as his resurrection meant a new beginning for mankind."[2]

It might be helpful to think about *who* wrote the words "Therefore, there is now no condemnation for those who are in Christ Jesus" (8:1). It is Paul, the former persecutor of Christians. Mark Batterson says Paul was essentially a terrorist by today's standards, and even after turning to Christ, he "could have allowed sinful memories to hold him hostage."[3] He could have allowed that guilt to make him feel unworthy to write letters like Romans or other works that now comprise a large chunk of the Bible. He could have felt too compromised to ever preach to *anyone* about anything. But that was not the reality he lived. He had been forgiven, his sin swept away, his past overruled. He was living in the kingdom Christ had ushered in, the era of the Holy Spirit, and he wanted everyone else to experience it too. No matter what you've done, who you are, or how guilty you feel, *there is now no condemnation* for those who are in Christ.

Romans 8:5–13

Life in Christ is not only about forgiveness, even though forgiveness of sins is a crucial aspect of the gospel. It also about life in the Spirit. Because of what Christ has ushered in, not only is our past no longer a problem, but our present is also transformed. The Holy Spirit lives in us. Verse 9 says Christ followers have moved from "the realm of the flesh" to "the realm of the Spirit." As Dunn explains, Paul isn't assuming that the process of salvation is finished but that it has started and "that the inner compulsion of God's Spirit has become the important factor at the level of primary motivation and enabling."[4]

Even the way we think about life changes. As verse 5 says, "Those who live according to the flesh have their minds set on what the flesh desires; but those who live in accordance with the Spirit have their minds set on what the Spirit desires." On what is your mind set? Notice the *intention* involved in this.

It's not that believers simply let their minds drift to the things of the Spirit if that's where their attention happens to take them. It's that they intentionally *set* their minds on the Spirit.

What fills your mind? I love teaching literature because it allows me to have those great works of fiction, poetry, and drama filling my mind—the words and images and scenes and dialogue from the greatest authors in history. I love to write about the Bible because that allows Scripture to permeate my mind. When I was a college student, one of my mentors said you know you're a true student of literature when these works become part of your life, not just something you read. In other words, your mind is set on them; they inhabit your mind. That is analogous to life in the Spirit. Having your mind set on the Spirit isn't only about *thinking*, of course. It's also about actions, and about *being*. You don't become a student of literature by thinking positive thoughts about literature. You have to read it. Your actions set your mind on it. What we set our mind on is connected to what we do, whom we spend time with, what we read and watch, what we allow to fill us.

How do we know if our mind is truly set on the Spirit? One question to consider is, what comes out of you when you are squeezed? Think of a sponge. Soak it in vinegar, and that's what's going to ooze out when you squeeze it. Soak it in lemon juice, and you get a much different result. What are you soaked in? I know people so soaked in sports that in just about any conversation you get involved in with them, something about a team or a playoff or an athlete is going to come out. I know other people so soaked in movies that the mere mention of a film title can squeeze lines of dialogue out of them, complete with their imitation of the actors' accents. Some people are so soaked in bitterness that if you squeeze them, they will ooze blame and cynicism and suspicion.

What if you're soaked in the Spirit? Think of people you know who are. What oozes out of them? Love! Also joy, peace, patience, kindness, goodness, faithfulness, gentleness, and self-control. Or, as Galatians 5:22–23 calls it, the fruit of the Spirit. That doesn't happen flawlessly, of course. We're all soaked in a mixture of things, and some of those less admirable substances will sometimes trickle out of even the most Spirit-soaked people. But those who bathe themselves in the Spirit by prayer, immersion in Scripture, and attention to acts of love are not going to be able to keep the Spirit from spilling out onto everyone around them.

Life in the Spirit sounds so good that you might think everybody would want it, but they don't. Their minds are set elsewhere. They may even be hostile to the Spirit or believe the Spirit doesn't exist. Peterson's translation of verse 9 in The Message says, "Anyone, of course, who has not welcomed this invisible but clearly present God, the Spirit of Christ, won't know what we're talking about." Those who are soaked in what Scripture calls "the flesh" believe that realm is the only reality. It will take the Holy Spirit's prompting to awaken them to the reality that lies outside that realm. Much of what we consider real, or normal, is dependent upon what we're immersed in.

To take an example from everyday life, it now seems normal for me to spend much of my day with my mind focused on some kind of electronic device, such as a laptop or cell phone. I use them for writing, phone calls, texts, emails, social media, maps, music, reading, news, movies, shopping, banking, classroom management, and many other activities. Conducting much of my life on those devices seems natural, and it's hard for me to imagine how I would function without them. They are where my mind lives. Yet I am also old enough to have lived in an era in which I *did* function without these devices, and quite happily. Those devices and all the services they provide did not always exist, but now it's hard for me to reconstruct in my mind exactly how I spent many of the hours of my day that I now spend on those devices, and how I managed to conduct my life effectively without them.

How did I manage to communicate with all the people I now quickly write to by email? I honestly can't remember in detail. I may have made more phone calls back then, but not that many more. And I certainly didn't write as many cards and letters and memos as I do emails. And email is only one part of my online life. But, however I managed it, that system seemed normal, and I remember that, when email first came along, I thought I would never need it. I didn't think I would need a smartphone when those came along, or social media, or many other aspects of digital life. Now I would dread those things being taken away. When my university issues me a new laptop every few years, I dread even the half day that I have to be without my computer as they switch my data from one machine to the other.

Just as digital life now seems natural and beneficial, even though it once seemed strange and unnecessary, so too life in the Spirit now seems obviously better than a life apart from God, even though before I became a Christian such a life seemed irrelevant or maybe even impossible. Each individual has the choice of whether to welcome God into one's life. From the outside, life in the Spirit is almost certain to look incomprehensible. The Holy Spirit helps us even with that skepticism, inviting us in. A rich spiritual life awaits, but accepting the invitation to it requires a leap of faith.

Romans 8:14–25

If we enter into this relationship with God, what is it like? What is God like? Is he like a mean boss, towering over us and waiting to yell at our first sign of failure? Is he like a slave owner? Is he like an angry drill sergeant? Is he like a distant relative from whom we might get a birthday card but little else?

Paul makes clear that we are adopted children—not in a distant, technical sense but in a close and loving way so that we can even call him by the intimate term for father, *Abba*. We, along with Christ the Son, are now not only children of the Father but also heirs. Our inheritance is eternity with him. We know our status not only intellectually but also because the Holy Spirit confirms it to us at the core of our being. As one of my favorite verses of Scripture says, "The Spirit himself testifies with our spirit that we are God's children" (v. 16).

That is beautiful and joyful, but it is not the whole story. There is more to being an heir and child than intimacy with God. As co-heirs with Christ, we share in his eternal, indescribably magnificent inheritance, but Paul reveals that we have that status as co-heirs "if indeed we share in his sufferings in order that we may also share in his glory" (v. 17). The tone of much of chapter 8 is celebratory, but Paul never forgets the fact that we have not yet arrived at our destination. We are still on the journey in this hostile world, and participating in Christ's suffering is an inescapable part of that journey.

The pain we experience as we share Christ's pain is not pointless. Paul compares our groaning—and the groaning of the entire creation—to the pain of childbirth. That pain leads to something good, but it is pain nevertheless. We should not expect to escape it, but knowing what it is makes it endurable because of what awaits us on the other side of it, if only we hang on until we get there. Sharing in Christ's suffering is something I don't like to think about. I don't want to share in *anyone's* suffering. I don't want to suffer. Paul—who shared in Christ's suffering enormously throughout his ministry, enduring persecution and repeated stints in jail and many other maladies—seems unsurprised by this painful element of his walk with Christ. He takes it in stride much better than I often do.

For me, times of suffering can be deceptive. When do I *feel* most loved by God and most unmistakably at the center of his purpose? Not when I suffer. On the contrary, when God is answering my prayers in the ways I want him to and allowing circumstances to work out the way I want them to, that's when I feel his love most forcefully. When I'm suffering, it's easy to doubt his love, or even his existence. But Paul is urging a shift in perspective about what suffering for Christ means. It is a sharing of what Christ has suffered, just as we will share in his glory. It's natural that I would want to look for a way out of suffering, but there isn't one.

What gets us through the shared suffering with Christ? How have Christians over the centuries been able to endure almost unfathomable pain, persecution, and death as followers of Christ? They have hope for the future. They have hope that their pain is not wasted. It is leading to something indescribably good. "I consider that our present sufferings are not worth comparing with the glory that will be revealed in us," says Paul (v. 18).

Depending on our circumstances and our frame of mind when we hear those words, they can either be the most hope-giving words possible, or they can make us want to punch a hole in the wall. During certain times of suffering, no amount of talk about how bright the future will be can penetrate our pain. We simply want it to stop *now*. But during calmer moments, if you think long and hard about what eternity really means—living forever in paradise with God, multiplying the intensity of the closest moments we have ever had with him, experiencing things beyond even the best things that have ever happened to us—then it can fortify us to endure more than we ever thought we could.

Think of how much of life consists of dealing with temporary difficulty or pain to reach something better later on. Athletes endure the pain and self-denial of training for months or years to win a single victory. Parents endure the sleepless nights, costs, and other endless hassles of child-rearing to experience the joy of relationship with their children. People wear themselves out on projects at work in order to please the boss or make a certain amount of money or enjoy the satisfaction of a job well done. If we are willing to endure so much for these good parts of a short, earthly life, then what are we willing to put up with for a life of uninterrupted joy that will last forever? When we can hold on to that eternal perspective, it can get us through many tough times, but what about when the pain overwhelms us?

Romans 8:26–30

"In the same way, the Spirit helps us in our weakness," writes Paul. "We do not know what we ought to pray for, but the Spirit himself intercedes for us through wordless groans" (v. 26). I know Romans 8:28 is the verse that ends up on all the posters and t-shirts, but if I were making the products, I would be tempted to put verse 26 on them instead. How reassuring it is for me to know that even when I get so low that I don't know what to pray for or don't even have the energy or will to pray for it, the Holy Spirit is still interceding for me with the Father.

Throughout my Christian life, I have heard people talk about "turning things over to God," releasing problems from our own hands and trusting God to deal with them. I've always had trouble with that. It's hard to let things go. I can pray about them, but I always want to work out the best solution, at least in my mind. It has taken me a long time to truly see this verse. *We do not know what we ought to pray for.*

Like most people I know, I spend a good chunk of my life problem-solving. Something pops up, and I attack it. The car breaks down, I get it fixed. Someone emails a request, I respond. I get sick, I go to the doctor. A class is coming up, I prepare for it. A bill comes due, I pay it. The list is endless. I often don't think to pray for those things. They are routine, and I feel like I can manage them. Some problems come along that I know are bigger than me, so I turn to prayer. Someone I love is terminally ill, so I pray for healing. Friends tell me they are getting divorced, so I pray for them. This list is also long, but at least I feel like I know what to pray for.

Sometimes my prayer time gets destroyed in spite of my best intentions. I have a list of people I pray for regularly, and my routine time for that prayer is during my morning run. I often start with that mental list as I run and then see where the prayer takes me. Some days that goes fine. I click through my list confidently, praying for each person, with time left over to let my mind wander. On other days, however, my mind is so overwhelmed by my own chaos or worries that I can barely make it through the first person on the list. As soon as I start to pray, these other worries wash away the prayer, and I'm off on a tangent of anger or worry or confusion. I try to bring myself back to prayer, and sometimes I get there for a few minutes, only to have the tide of my own distracted thoughts wash it away again. Before long, I find myself needing to ask for prayer just to be able to pray. I need the Holy Spirit to do my praying *for* me, and also to hear my prayer.

The good news is that's what he is already doing. "The Spirit intercedes for God's people in accordance with the will of God" (v. 27b). At times I can't pray the way I should because my own selfishness blinds me, or fear twists my perspective, or I lack enough information and insight to see the big picture of my life. My own prayer matters, but how spiritually steadying it is for me to know that prayer doesn't depend only on *my* ability to do it. I always have someone far greater praying for me.

God is constantly at work not only in prayer but also in circumstances. That is where the famous Romans 8:28 comes in. Just as God doesn't put all the burden of prayer on us but actually participates in it as the Holy Spirit intercedes for us, so God doesn't simply let circumstances take any pointless direction they might otherwise take without God's influence. Some people use the promise of 8:28, that "in all things God works for the good of those who love him, who have been called according to his purpose," as a kind of denial of the pain of life, as if the bad things aren't really bad. However, Paul does not deny the reality of suffering. Remember, by the time he writes the words in 8:28, he has already established the truth that being a co-heir with Christ means we will share in his suffering. If you are looking toward 8:28 as a verse to brush away suffering, you are looking in the wrong place.

As we know, much of life is about dealing with problems, limitations, disappointments, persecutions, obstacles, injustices, heartbreak. Romans 8:28 does not diminish that pain. It instead sees it in a wider framework. For those who do not believe in God but instead interpret the world from a purely materialistic perspective, suffering exists apart from any larger framework. It has no meaning. It simply is.

For Christians, however, suffering can be seen as part of a cosmic battle between good and evil. God's intentions for us, his human creations, are good, but human-chosen sin has temporarily interrupted that good. The death of Jesus on the cross has set things right and made a way for our salvation, which we may freely accept or reject. For those who accept this gift of salvation and are called according to God's purpose, suffering is not an end in itself but a painful element in a process that God will bend toward redemption, just as Jesus's death on the cross did not *stop* with that pain of death but instead worked toward the good of our salvation.

God's impulse toward redemption is so powerful that he takes even the worst things and makes them function toward this purpose. These worst things are bad, but that badness is not the final word. Worst things are an ingredient that, mixed with other ingredients, will ultimately form something good. They are like dirt. It is not good to eat, it is messy, it can clog machinery, it can turn to mud and ruin a carpet or rage through a house in a storm or cause all kinds of other problems. But dirt, when joined with the right mixture of seeds, water, warmth, and sunshine, can grow enormous amounts of good things to eat. We would all be dead without it. God is adept at taking even the worst things and using them as ingredients to form something that is ultimately good.

God's perspective is eternal, so sometimes we don't see the good in this life. It may come to fruition generations from now, or it may not be clear until eternity. As Douglas Moo points out in his commentary on Romans, "The 'good' God may have in mind may involve the next life entirely. He may take us out of a secure, well-paying job in order to shake us out of a materialistic lifestyle that does not honor biblical priorities, and we may never have as good a job again." Or, Moo adds, God may want to get us out of a marriage engagement in order to make us available for a ministry that would be prohibitive for a married person.[5]

It's true that in many cases the good that God is working out will be hard for us to see, but we also should not overlook the number of times in life when we *do* see God's hand guiding circumstances to a good we never could have imagined. If the good that God is working became evident *only* in eternity, it might become hard for us to believe in Romans 8:28, but one reason the verse holds such power for many believers is that occasionally we *can* look at circumstances and sense the evidence that God has been there, that his loving fingerprints are on a situation. Have you ever prayed fervently that a particular relationship will work out, only to have it implode and leave you heartbroken? Yet, as the months and years go by, you see how destructive it would have been to your life if God had answered that prayer.

Have you ever begged God to grant you a particular job, only to see it go to someone else while you are left stuck and bewildered? Yet later you see that God was working out an opportunity you never could have foreseen that fits you even better. Have you ever had what some people call a "divine appointment," when you run into just the right person at just the right time, or when you are there for someone at just the right time? Have you ever experienced what some Christians call a "God thing," when circumstances align in a way that seems too perfect for mere coincidence, making you think God must be in it?

Romans 8:31–38

Imagine that you are Paul, having just written this soaring and intense portion of your letter that, centuries later, will be called Romans 8. How do you conclude this section? It's not as if you have delivered only good news in this chapter. You have talked about sharing in Christ's suffering, which will make up a significant portion of life. But you have also spoken of an intimate relationship with the Holy Spirit, the end of condemnation because of what Christ has done, and the hope of a glorious future in eternity.

Paul could simply stop right there and let that message speak for itself. But instead he pauses and asks, "What, then, shall we say in response to these things?" (v. 31a). His answer: "If God is for us, who can be against us?" (v. 32b). Paul isn't simply completing a thought in these final verses of the chapter. He is exulting in a God who loves us so extravagantly. It's as if, despite whatever hardships he sees all around him, he catches a glimpse of where he stands in the bigger picture of God's love, and he can't help but break out in cheer and praise to God. God is for us! Think of the implications of that. If it's really true—and Paul believes to his core that it is—then, as he declares in verse 37, "we are more than conquerors through him who loved us." *Conquerors*. We suffer, but we conquer. Individually and as an international church, we face every imaginable difficulty—persecution, poverty, famine, war—but even the worst of those things does not separate us from God's love. We may look pretty ragged at the moment, but victory is on its way.

Romans 8 may be one of the most influential chapters in the Bible because it does not ask small questions. It asks the biggest questions of all. Where does all this end? Is there hope? Where are we headed? Does suffering have meaning? Do we ultimately win or lose? The hope of Romans 8 is that, in Christ, our condemnation is swept away, we are adopted as co-heirs with Christ, and we are headed toward an eternity in which our pain will be redeemed. God is for us.

Notes

1. Mark Batterson, *If: Trading Your If Only Regrets for God's What If Possibilities* (Grand Rapids: Baker Publishing Group, 2015), 15.

2. James D. G. Dunn, *Word Biblical Commentary: Romans 1–8*, Vol. 38 (Dallas: Word Books, 1988), 439.

3. Batterson, *If,* 33.

4. Dunn, *Romans 1–8*, 444.

5. Douglas Moo, *Romans: The NIV Application Commentary* (Grand Rapids: Zondervan, 2000), 278.

Digging Deeper

1. Romans 8 includes some of the most beautiful and celebrated verses in all of the Bible. If you could choose only two that have the most profound impact on you, what would they be? Describe why you find these verses so powerful.

2. When it comes to prayer, Romans 8:26 says the Holy Spirit "helps us in our weakness. We do not know what we ought to pray for, but the Spirit himself intercedes for us through wordless groans." In what ways do you need to rely on God not only for the answers to prayer but also for the prayers themselves? Why would we not know what we ought to pray for?

3. Romans 8:28 is one of the most famous verses of the Bible. What are some ways you have heard it misused? What is your understanding of this verse in the context of this section of Romans?

Go to https://www.thefoundrypublishing.com/12NT/LeaderGuide for a free downloadable leader's guide that includes more questions for reflection as well as activities for use in a small group setting.

Jesus's Most Important Days

10

Madonna and Child // Francisco Bayeu y Subias // c. 1734-1795

A Child Is Born

[4] *So Joseph also went up from the town of Nazareth in Galilee to Judea, to Bethlehem the town of David, because he belonged to the house and line of David.* [5] *He went there to register with Mary, who was pledged to be married to him and was expecting a child.* [6] *While they were there, the time came for the baby to be born,* [7] *and she gave birth to her firstborn, a son. She wrapped him in cloths and placed him in a manger, because there was no guest room available for them.*

[8] *And there were shepherds living out in the fields nearby, keeping watch over their flocks at night.* [9] *An angel of the Lord appeared to them, and the glory of the Lord shone around them, and they were terrified.* [10] *But the angel said to them, "Do not be afraid. I bring you good news that will cause great joy for all the people.* [11] *Today in the town of David a Savior has been born to you; he is the Messiah, the Lord.* [12] *This will be a sign to you: You will find a baby wrapped in cloths and lying in a manger."*

—Luke 2:4–12

ENTIRE INDUSTRIES THRIVE on a holiday that presumably celebrates the birth of a baby to a poor family in Bethlehem two thousand years ago.

Take Christmas trees. According to the National Christmas Tree Association (yes, there is such a thing), in the United States alone, up to 30 million real Christmas trees are sold each year, and 350 million Christmas trees are growing on 15,000 tree farms in all 50 states and Canada. More than 100,000 people have jobs in this industry.[1]

How about Christmas cards? In the social media age, do people still bother sending paper cards through the mail? According to the Greeting Card Association, people still send about 1.6 billion Christmas cards each year, spending around $2 billion to do so. That number far outranks the second-biggest greeting card holiday, Valentine's Day, which generates only one-tenth that number of card sales.[2]

Does all that spending leave enough money to still buy lights for the house and inflatable snowmen and Santa Clauses? Sure! Americans spend about $6 billion on those things too.[3]

All those billions of dollars are small change compared to how much people spend on the really big item, Christmas presents. American adults spend around $800 each on Christmas presents each year. In 2016 more than 154 million people went shopping on Thanksgiving weekend alone, and retail spending for November and December of that year added up to about $650 billion.[4]

The birth of Jesus Christ as told in the Bible has changed the world, but the holiday that is devoted to it, Christmas, does almost as much to obscure that momentous event as it does to reveal it. When my kids were little and liked to shake the presents under the tree to try to figure out what they were, we sometimes wrapped small presents inside a series of larger boxes. The kids would unwrap one box only to find another wrapped one inside it, and another inside that, until they finally reached the one that held their gift. Often it feels as if the true Christmas lies hidden inside layers of extraneous fluff.

In some ways the way we treat Christmas reminds me of the way most Christians experienced Bible stories hundreds of years ago, before they had their own Bibles or could even read the ones that existed. People relied on artistic representations of the biblical stories and on sermons and plays to bring the stories to life. Christmas today is something like that for many people. It's not that Jesus has been completely removed from Christmas—it's that his role in it has to compete with so many other layers of what the holiday has come to mean. We still see him in the nativity scenes on our coffee tables and in live nativity scenes in front of churches, with real people and animals acting out the parts. Children still dress up like Mary and Joseph and wise men and shepherds to act out plays in church. Films and cartoons still show the story, and greeting cards depict scenes from Jesus's birth.

But the birth of Jesus is a biblical story that long ago broke out of the confines of the church and became not only a religious celebration but also a secular one. That secularization means that more people will learn about Jesus and be reminded of him every year, but on the downside, the story they hear will almost certainly be corrupted and mixed with many extraneous elements. Christmas serves not only as a celebration of the Christ child but also as an excuse for Walmart to advertise Black Friday sales on televisions and coffeemakers and socks.

Even in Christian homes, where the birth of Christ is revered, the sacred and secular become intertwined. At the same time that I unpack the nativity set from our garage each Christmas, I also pull out the lights to put on our Christmas tree because we all know that the Christmas tree shows up in the story of Jesus's birth when—well, there is no Christmas tree in the Bible. That tradition is a carryover from Roman times. But at least our gifts *under* the tree are biblical, right? We give gifts because the wise men did? Sorry, that's just an after-the-fact justification for another pre-Christian practice. With all these added-on elements, I'm glad we at least know that December 25 is the actual day that Jesus was born—except that we don't. That date was settled on by church leaders after years of debate and varying proposals. It may also shock you to know that certain other Christmas favorites are not in the Bible, such as Rudolph, Santa Claus, stockings hung by the fire, the Grinch, mistletoe, fruitcake, and candy canes.

Even when we turn to the actual biblical narrative, errors abound in how we often depict it. The nativity scene that sat atop our television set during all my growing-up years included the three wise men (always three) standing right there with the shepherds and staring at the baby Jesus in his manger. My job as a kid was to unwrap the plaster characters and place them in their correct spots in and around the little wooden stable. Imagine my surprise when I learned that the shepherds and wise men were never together at all! The shepherds saw baby Jesus in the manger (Luke 2:16), but the wise men, whose number is not specified, didn't find the child until quite a bit later, when Mary, Joseph, and Jesus were living in a house and Jesus was presumably no longer sleeping in a manger (Matthew 2:11).

It gets worse. As if it were not bad enough that I had to remove the wise men from my nativity stable, some scholars believe I need to get rid of the stable itself because Jesus wasn't born in one. Even though we were always told Jesus had to be born in the stable and placed in the manger because there was no room at the inn, the word for "inn," *kataluma*, might be better translated as "guest room," and it might be referring to a spare room in a private home, such as a relative's home, rather than a public inn like a hotel. *Kataluma* is the same word used for "upper room" in the Last Supper story, and it's different from the word for the public inn used in the Good Samaritan story. So it's likely that there was no room for Mary and Joseph in the guest room of a relative's house.

As theologian Ian Paul explains, families in that era often lived in houses with one main room and then a guest room at the back or space for guests on the roof. "The family living area would usually have hollows in the ground, filled with straw, in the living area, where the animals would feed."[5] So the animals might be just outside the main living area of the house, not in some lonely stable. That space might have been available for guests if the guest room was already taken. That makes sense, but it certainly complicates my nativity set.

One drawback to the fact that the story of Jesus's birth is tied so inextricably to such a muddled holiday is that it may cause us to compartmentalize this event from the rest of the message and story of Christianity. We dust off the story of Christ's birth each December when we haul the Christmas decorations out of the garage, and we put it away again about a month later, never to contemplate it again until the following year. Even during that month or so when we celebrate it, the way we think of it often sentimentalizes it. The birth of the baby is more cute than spiritually significant. Mary and Joseph huddled around the sweet baby in the manger/crib gets all mixed up with our own families huddled around eggnog and presents in front of the fireplace. Jesus is merely one more familiar Christmas character, like the Grinch or Santa Claus, rather than the Son of God, Son of Man, radical Savior of the world.

Set aside the trappings of Christmas for a moment to see the Christ who is at the center of it. What was the significance of the birth of that baby Jesus? The eternal Son of God, while remaining divine, also took on a human nature. As Philippians 2:6–8 describes it, Jesus, "being in very nature God, did not consider equality with God something to be used to his own advantage; rather, he made himself nothing by taking the very nature of a servant, being made in human likeness. And being found in appearance as a man, he humbled himself by becoming obedient to death—even death on a cross!" In that statement Paul connects Christmas with the crucifixion, something it's easy to forget to do. Of the many miracles of Christmas, the most crucial one is that God came to us as a human being. Jesus advocates for us before the Father. He is our Savior and High Priest. Hebrews 4 says we should hold firmly to our faith, "For we do not have a high priest who is unable to empathize with our weaknesses, but we have one who has been tempted in every way, just as we are—yet he did not sin" (v. 15).

The Many Stories of Christmas

Jesus is at the center of the Christmas story, of course, but his story is not the only one that gets buried under the mountains of tinsel and candy canes and wrapping paper. The biblical story of Jesus's incarnation also includes stories of other fascinating people whose lives have much to inspire us. Some of them don't get turned into plastic characters that are given a spot in nativity scenes, and no child gets to portray them in annual Christmas plays, but their stories of faith are instructive to those who pay attention. Two of my favorites are Zechariah and Elizabeth.

In the months before the angel Gabriel came to Mary to announce that she would give birth to Jesus, the angel first went to Zechariah to announce that his wife, Elizabeth, would give birth to John the Baptist, whose work would prepare people for Jesus's ministry. Zechariah and Elizabeth were old and had been unable to conceive a child. They surely must have given up on the idea by the time the angel arrived. Zechariah was doing his duty as a priest in the temple when Gabriel came to say, "Do not be afraid, Zechariah; your prayer has been heard. Your wife Elizabeth will bear you a son, and you are to call him John" (Luke 1:13).

Zechariah, naturally, struggled to comprehend this news. His prayer had been heard? Would he have still been praying that prayer as an old man? He says, "How can I be sure of this? I am an old man and my wife is well along in years" (v. 18). A reasonable question, but it was not what the angel wanted to hear. These were the days of miracles, and Zechariah was right in the middle of them. He may have expected to live out his life quietly, disappointed at the lack of children in a culture in which having them was seen as a key sign of God's blessing. Little did Zechariah suspect that he would play such a big role in God's story of redemption for the world. When his moment came, he wasn't quite ready for it, so Gabriel told him he wouldn't be able to speak until the child was born.

Zechariah got the news first, but Elizabeth's life was also rocked by the happy turmoil of this miracle. She had been looked down upon because of her lack of children, but now she not only was pregnant with a child who would become one of the most important men of the faith, but she also got to share this news with Mary, who visited her while also pregnant with Jesus. Elizabeth's baby leapt in her womb when Mary came.

Once Elizabeth gave birth to John, Zechariah could speak again, and he spoke a prophecy that beautifully encompassed not only what his own son, John the Baptist, would do but also the significance of Jesus's arrival to save us: "And you, my child, will be called a prophet of the Most High; for you will go on before the Lord to prepare the way for him, to give his people the knowledge of salvation through the forgiveness of their sins, because of the tender mercy of our God, by which the rising sun will come to us from heaven to shine on those living in darkness and in the shadow of death, to guide our feet into the path of peace" (vv. 76–79).

Even the Genealogies Tell a Story

Two sections of the Christmas story that most people skip entirely when they celebrate Jesus's birth are the genealogies that appear in Matthew 1 and

Luke 3. I vividly remember helping my young son memorize Luke 2 to recite at a church Christmas play, but I don't remember hearing *any* child in *any* Christmas event recite the genealogies. Most people are no more likely to read those than they would read the fine print on their credit card agreement. Should anyone really care that Elihud was the father of Eleazar and Eleazar the father of Matthan?

Today many of us cannot even trace back our *own* lineage more than a few generations, so why do we need to know Jesus's ancestry going back to Abraham? New Testament professor Jason Hood ties the genealogies to the spiritual importance of *waiting* for God to fulfill his promises and to work out his purposes. Abraham, who is at the beginning of the genealogy in Matthew, lived more than two thousand years before Jesus. God promised Abraham the whole world would be blessed through him and his offspring (Gen. 12:1–7). Much further down in the genealogy is David. God "promised David that his son—who would also be God's son—would rule on the throne, and that even the nations would one day be under his reign (2 Sam. 7:8–15). He also promised a New Covenant and a New Creation after the disaster of Exile (Jer. 31:31–34)."[6]

The genealogies, far from being some kind of boring small print to skip over, show Christians today that God often takes a long time to fulfill his purposes. We, like so many of those names on the lists, may see none or only part of that fulfillment during our own lifetimes, but that doesn't mean God is not at work. The genealogies help readers take the long view of God's story. The birth of Jesus is a high point of that story, but still today we participate in its continuation as we look forward to Christ's *second* coming and the new heaven and new earth of eternity.

Hood also points out that Matthew includes four gentiles in his genealogy: Tamar, Rahab, Ruth, and Uriah. Each of these outsiders was "widely considered to have been a convert who left the idols of the nations and was transformed into a righteous follower of Israel's God. Each of these gentiles is a down payment on God's plan to bless every family of the world."[7] The genealogies are filled with imperfect, troubled people who needed God's rescue just as much as we do. After centuries of waiting, Jesus came.

A Brave and Daring Young Woman

While it may not be surprising that people have trouble incorporating genealogies and certain other obscure elements of the Christmas story into their traditions, even one of the central figures of the story—Mary, the mother of Jesus—gets distorted and in a certain sense diminished by the Christmas holiday. Mary, of course, is one of the most well-known and revered women in history. She holds an exalted place in the Catholic Church in particular. But in the Protestant tradition, Mary becomes little more than the plaster character in a nativity set. There she sits wrapped in blue garments, looking serenely and adoringly toward the little baby Jesus in the straw-filled manger. That is also how Mary is depicted in countless paintings and sculptures over the centuries. That certainly is one aspect of her story, but Mary did far more than gaze lovingly at her baby. This young mother also showed tremendous courage and action. When the evil ruler Herod was hell-bent on killing her son, Mary and her husband took their baby and fled to Egypt—surely a difficult, expensive, and scary journey.

Mary didn't seek fame or influence. The angel came to *her* as a complete surprise. She was minding her own business, living with the integrity of life that most women of her culture experienced. She was betrothed to a man named Joseph. The angel Gabriel arrived with good news. He told her she was highly favored by God. The Lord was with her. Who wouldn't want to hear that? But Mary was "greatly troubled" by the words, and her concern only grew when she heard the stunning plan the angel set before her. She would give birth to "the Son of the Most High. The Lord God will give him the throne of his father David, and he will reign over Jacob's descendants forever; his kingdom will never end" (Luke 1:32–33).

That is the weighty and historic responsibility this young woman was asked to assume. She had a few questions! How could this happen since she was a virgin? The answer was so unusual that it could have hardly been reassuring: "The Holy Spirit will come on you, and the power of the Most High will overshadow you. So the holy one to be born will be called the Son of God" (v. 35).

Yet Mary didn't run. She didn't make excuses or find a way out. With tremendous faith in God, she accepted the burden and privilege that had been placed on her. She accepted whatever gossip, difficulty, confusion, and pain would come. She *acted* to raise this child who was unlike any other. The tone of Mary's song that is recorded in Scripture, now known as the *Magnificat*, is one of gratitude, not fear or resistance: "My soul glorifies the Lord and my spirit rejoices in God my Savior, for he has been mindful of the humble state of his servant. From now on all generations will call me blessed, for the Mighty One has done great things for me—holy is his name. His mercy extends to those who fear him, from generation to generation" (vv. 46–50).

Mary is a role model of faith—Jesus's mother but also his follower, who ultimately had to watch him be executed. The man who became Mary's husband, Joseph, also followed the Lord's leading at great personal risk. When Mary became pregnant before their marriage, he planned to end the arrangement as the law called for, but he intended to do it quietly, lovingly, so she would not be disgraced. As with Mary, Joseph had to put his trust in the unlikely words of an angel, who reassured him that this child was of the Holy Spirit and that the marriage should go forward. Joseph did act in faith and obedience, even though it meant he would soon have to leave everything familiar behind and flee to Egypt with his young family in order to escape the murderous Herod.

The Many Messages of Christmas

The true message of Jesus's birth is always in danger of being obscured. However, that doesn't mean that all the extra messages that have accumulated around Christmas are bad. Some of the added layers are full of love, hope, and childlike wonder. Some of our best stories are Christmas stories, even though they have nothing specifically to do with the birth of Christ. Think how diminished our culture would be without Charles Dickens's *A Christmas Carol* and the many adaptations of that classic. How many millions of times have viewers seen *It's a Wonderful Life* and been moved and inspired?

The stories that emerge at Christmas are different from what people are drawn to the rest of the year. What is the message of the typical Christmas movie? We should care more about *people* and *relationships* than *things*. We should slow down and appreciate the small joys of life. We should focus more on giving than on competing. Those are Christian messages, even if they are not specifically about the birth of Christ. How much better might the world be if those were the messages that hit us more consistently year-round?

It is often said that the Christmas story appears in only two of the Gospel accounts, Matthew and Luke. Certainly those are the only two with shepherds, a manger, an inn, wise men, and all the elements of the Christmas story that we have come to see as traditional. However, the Gospel of John also contains its own brief, but profound, story of the movement of God into the flesh of a human being. In one sense the whole Christmas story is summarized in

John 1:14: "The Word became flesh and made his dwelling among us. We have seen his glory, the glory of the one and only Son, who came from the Father, full of grace and truth." Christmas is about the incarnation, the eternal Son of God becoming human without ceasing to be God. He came to be a sacrifice for the sins of humanity. He is a sinless human being and fully God.

The Christmas story continues to grip the world. It is a profound story, yet one that even a child can understand. A baby is born. The story contains miraculous elements—the angels, the star, the fact that the baby is human but also God—but it is also the story of a humble birth, the celebration of a new child born into a family. That part has been repeated millions of times. In some ways it was a birth like any other. We understand it and can relate to it. But in other ways that will change lives for eternity, it stands out from every other birth in history.

Notes

1. National Christmas Tree Association, "Quick Tree Facts," http://www.realchristmas trees.org/dnn/Education/Quick-Tree-Facts.

2. Ethan Wolff-Mann, "This Is How Much People Still Spend on Christmas Cards," *Money* magazine, December 14, 2015, http://money.com/money/4148180/christmas-cards-spending -2015/.

3. Madeleine Scinto, "Americans Are Spending A Whopping $6 Billion on Christmas Decorations This Year," *Business Insider*, December 7, 2011, https://www.businessinsider.com /americans-are-spending-a-record-6-billion-on-christmas-decorations-2011-12.

4. Cristina Silva, "Christmas Spending 2016: How Much Money Do Americans Spend on Gifts?" *International Business Times*, December 14, 2016, https://www.ibtimes.com/christmas -spending-2016-how-much-money-do-americans-spend-gifts-2460727.

5. Ian Paul, "Once More: Jesus Was Not Born in a Stable," *Psephizo*, December 3, 2018, https://www.psephizo.com/biblical-studies/once-more-jesus-was-not-born-in-a-stable/.

6. Jason Hood, "Jesus's Family Tree Shows Us He Is Worth the Wait," *Christianity Today*, December 29, 2016, https://www.christianitytoday.com/ct/2016/december-web-only/genealogy -in-matthew-waiting.html.

7. Hood, "Jesus's Family Tree."

Digging Deeper

1. Does the fact that many churches talk about and study the birth of Christ only during the season of Christmas diminish or distort its importance in the Christian faith? Would there be some value in studying these Christmas passages at other times of year too?

2. The birth of Jesus is the central story of Christmas, but this chapter also sheds light on other biblical elements that are related to that story, such as the genealogies and the story of Zechariah and Elizabeth. What biblical story or passage connected to the birth of Christ stands out to you as particularly meaningful?

3. Christmas trees, candy canes, Santa movies, and many other unbiblical elements have been layered onto the biblical story of Jesus's birth. That might obscure Jesus's story in some ways, but does it also make some people, especially those who are not Christians, more likely to hear about Jesus? What overall impact do you think the cultural appropriation of Christmas has had on the Christian message?

Go to https://www.thefoundrypublishing.com/12NT/LeaderGuide for a free downloadable leader's guide that includes more questions for reflection as well as activities for use in a small group setting.

11

Last Supper // Jacopo Robusti Tintoretto // c. 1518-1594

The Last Supper and Gethsemane

[26] *While they were eating, Jesus took bread, and when he had given thanks, he broke it and gave it to his disciples, saying, "Take and eat; this is my body."*

[27] *Then he took a cup, and when he had given thanks, he gave it to them, saying, "Drink from it, all of you.* [28] *This is my blood of the covenant, which is poured out for many for the forgiveness of sins.* [29] *I tell you, I will not drink from this fruit of the vine from now on until that day when I drink it new with you in my Father's kingdom."*

[36] *Then Jesus went with his disciples to a place called Gethsemane, and he said to them, "Sit here while I go over there and pray."* [37] *He took Peter and the two sons of Zebedee along with him, and he began to be sorrowful and troubled.* [38] *Then he said to them, "My soul is overwhelmed with sorrow to the point of death. Stay here and keep watch with me."*

[39] *Going a little farther, he fell with his face to the ground and prayed, "My Father, if it is possible, may this cup be taken from me. Yet not as I will, but as you will."*

[40] *Then he returned to his disciples and found them sleeping. "Couldn't you men keep watch with me for one hour?" he asked Peter.* [41] *"Watch and pray so that you will not fall into temptation. The spirit is willing, but the flesh is weak."*

[42] *He went away a second time and prayed, "My Father, if it is not possible for this cup to be taken away unless I drink it, may your will be done."*

[43] *When he came back, he again found them sleeping, because their eyes were heavy.* [44] *So he left them and went away once more and prayed the third time, saying the same thing.*

[45] *Then he returned to the disciples and said to them, "Are you still sleeping and resting? Look, the hour has come, and the Son of Man is delivered into the hands of sinners.* [46] *Rise! Let us go! Here comes my betrayer!"*

—Matthew 26:26–29, 36–46

IF YOU SEARCHED for the most momentous twenty-four-hour period in history, few—if any—days could compare to the hours leading up to the crucifixion of Jesus Christ. Much of the Christian message is embodied within the details of that story. And it *is* a story. It is not only a set of principles, or arguments, or declarations. Things happened. Afterward, the world was never the same.

Many people have never read that story in the Bible itself, but almost everyone has at least some knowledge of it. They have seen a cross and know it is a Christian symbol. They have heard the term "Last Supper" and know it refers to Jesus's final meal with his disciples.

These closing chapters will focus on the final twenty-four hours of Jesus's earthly life by shining a light on key moments: the supper he shared with the twelve flawed men who were his closest friends, the agonizing hours of prayer that followed in a nearby garden, and the horrific death Jesus suffered when he was nailed to a wooden torture device. But, of course, his death was not the end of the story. Another chapter will celebrate what happened three days later, when Jesus rose from the dead.

A cup. A piece of bread. A cross. An empty tomb. These are the symbols that have represented Christianity for centuries. The story in which they appear has been reenacted, painted, preached, filmed, criticized, denied, censored, and revered. Its influence on the world is too momentous to ignore.

The Most Famous Supper in History

The Lord's Supper has been reenacted billions of times around the earth in the two thousand years since Jesus and his disciples sat down for that meal. The disciples were caught up in their own crisis that night, and it would have been beyond their imagination to realize that one day this meal would be considered so important that it would be celebrated even *off* the Earth, on the faraway moon above them.

When human beings first landed on the moon on July 20, 1969, one of the astronauts who walked on its surface, Buzz Aldrin, knew the historical significance of what he was doing that day. He wanted to find the right symbol to mark the occasion. He later wrote, "I wondered if it might be possible to take Communion on the moon, symbolizing the thought that God was revealing himself there too, as man reached out into the universe."[1] He was allowed to take a few personal items on the flight, so he decided to take the bread and wine and a small silver cup his pastor gave him. The lunar module landed at 3:30 p.m. on July 20. As he prepared to walk on the surface of the moon, Aldrin took Communion during a radio blackout period. As he describes it, "In the one-sixth gravity of the moon the wine curled slowly and gracefully up the side of the cup. It was interesting to think that the very first liquid ever poured on the moon, and the first food eaten there, were Communion elements."[2]

Few examples of people partaking in the Lord's Supper are that dramatic. In fact, one of the beautiful aspects of this ritual is that it does *not* need a dramatic setting or occasion in which to be carried out. Throughout history, and across the world today, it has happened on battlefields, in hospitals, at bedsides, in huts, in stadiums, in monasteries, in universities, on ships, and in countless churches of every imaginable Christian tradition. This sacrament has been carried out in hundreds of languages in just about every nation that exists.

The Last Supper goes by different names—the Eucharist, Mass, Communion, the Lord's Supper—and there are significant differences in what various branches of Christianity believe about this sacrament and how they include it in their worship. The scope of this chapter is not large enough to consider all those variations. Catholics handle it differently than Nazarenes, who treat it differently than Lutherans, Anglicans, or Pentecostals. Even within some of those denominations, individual congregations have a variety of ways they conduct and think about the Eucharist. Some believe the bread and wine become the actual body and blood of Christ. Others believe Jesus's body and blood are present "in, with, and under" the elements. Some believe Jesus is *spiritually* present with the bread and wine. Still others say that the Lord's Supper is a remembrance of Jesus's final meal.

As Disaster Looms, Jesus Shares a Meal

Considering the importance of this meal in Christian history, it may be surprising to note how humble the original supper was. It did not take place in a palace. There were no servants scurrying around, taking care of every detail and making sure everyone was served. That's not how Jesus operated. When the disciples came in with dirty feet, no one was there to wash them, so Jesus broke protocol and washed their feet himself. Even though his betrayal, arrest, and death were mere hours away, and even though Jesus knew his betrayer was right there in the room with him, he still kept teaching his disciples about love and servanthood right to the end.

The Lord's Supper took place in the upper room of someone's home, a person not named in the Bible. The disciples had found this room by following Jesus's mysterious instructions to follow a man carrying a jar of water and ask the owner of the house he entered, "The Teacher asks: Where is my guest room, where I may eat the Passover with my disciples?" (Mark 14:14). The man would show them to a large upper room furnished and ready. There they would prepare the Passover. Tension was high as the disciples followed those instructions and made preparations in the room to which they were led. The plot against Jesus by the religious authorities was approaching a climax, and Jesus did not try to hide this from his disciples. He had bluntly told them, "As you know, the Passover is two days away—and the Son of Man will be handed over to be crucified" (Matthew 26:2).

The Lord's Supper was not the first time Jesus put a meal at the center of his ministry and teaching about the kingdom of God. Henri Nouwen, in his book on the prodigal son parable, says that in Jesus's teaching, the "invitation to a meal is an invitation to intimacy with God. This is especially true at the Last Supper, shortly before Jesus's death."[3] Although the meals are invitations to intimacy with God, those invitations are not always accepted. In the prodigal son parable, the father throws an elaborate celebratory meal for his younger son who has returned, but the older refuses to go in, despite his father's pleading.

In another of Jesus's parables about the kingdom of God, the king prepares a wedding feast for his son, but the invited guests refuse to come. They have better things to do, with one going off to his field and another to his business. The king sends servants to go out into the streets to invite anyone they can find so the wedding hall would be full (Matthew 22:2-14). God is opening the kingdom and inviting people in, but as the parables show, not everyone is eager to accept God's invitation to intimacy and celebration.

Jesus's supper with the disciples on that historic night was also a complex mixture of intimacy and tension. What he did and said with the bread and cup would reverberate through the centuries. He was sharing something of enormous significance with them. "And he said to them, 'I have eagerly desired to eat this Passover with you before I suffer. For I tell you, I will not eat it again until it finds fulfillment in the kingdom of God'" (Luke 22:15-16). On the other hand, he also told them that one of them sitting there would betray him, which filled them with doubt and sorrow.

Another discordant note was thrown into the evening when a dispute broke out over which of them would be considered the greatest. Jesus once again had to teach them—at this late hour in his ministry!—that serving one another, not worldly ambition or greatness, is what his kingdom is all about.

The meal ended with a hymn. Then they walked to the garden of Gethsemane, with Jesus's arrest, torture, and crucifixion imminent. The Lord's Supper was like some of the family meals many of us have been part of, where love and deep connection wrestle with conflict and troubled relationships. Communion now often takes place in reverent settings, in hushed, stained-glass-windowed sanctuaries filled with polite prayers and soothing music. That is certainly appropriate, considering the profound significance of the sacrament. But I love the fact that the original Last Supper took place not when circumstances were tranquil but on the worst night of Jesus's life. Jesus still invites us into intimate connection with him in any circumstance, whether we're at our best or at our worst. He gave the cup and the bread that night to men he knew would flee from him only hours later.

Leonardo da Vinci Interprets a Moment

Ask people what picture comes to mind when they hear the term "Last Supper," and some might mention Leonardo da Vinci's painting, which he painted on the refectory wall of the Dominican convent of the Santa Maria delle Grazie in Milan from 1495 to 1498. Of all the moments the artist could have chosen to capture from that meal, Leonardo chose to depict the disciples' reaction to Jesus's statement, "Truly I tell you, one of you will betray me" (Matthew 26:21). The painting, which has been restored numerous times and also narrowly escaped destruction in World War II, shows in detail each disciple's troubled reaction to the idea that one of them will betray Jesus.

Although the painting in many ways is not realistic—the supper almost certainly did not take place with everyone sitting on one side of the table, and people of that era generally reclined when they ate—it defines that important moment in Scripture for countless people. Its popularity has not been harmed by the fact that the painting shows a low point in the meal rather than the breaking of bread or passing of the cup that now define how the meal is reenacted in Communion.

Leonardo's painting is one of the most copied religious paintings of all time. It is celebrated not only as fine art but has also been reproduced on novelty items like posters, pillows, wrapping paper, skateboards, postage stamps, clipboards, stationery, luggage tags, coffee mugs, comforters, and baseball caps. Some of those reproductions certainly sound irreverent—not only toward a classic work of art but also toward the sacred moment depicted in it—but it is yet another sign of the inescapable significance of that singular meal, both in history and in the lives of people today.

Jesus's Meal Connects Past, Present, and Future

One of the remarkable facts about the Last Supper is that it points us both backward and forward in time. Jesus did not choose a random night to have this meal. Jesus shared the *Passover* meal with his disciples, which looks back to the time of Moses, when God set his people free from Egyptian slavery. Moses had demanded that Pharaoh free the Hebrews, but the heart-hardened leader of Egypt kept refusing. A series of plagues would temporarily make Pharaoh agree to let the people go, but then he would change his mind and refuse. The culminating plague took the lives of every firstborn in Egyptian households, and for Hebrew households, only blood on their doorposts from a sacrificial lamb kept death away.

Now, as Jesus met with his disciples on this momentous evening, his blood was about to be shed as a sacrifice to cover the sin of all humanity. He would transform the Passover meal into something new. From that night on it would commemorate his shed blood and broken body. Tim Stafford says that if Jesus wanted to emphasize only forgiveness of sins in this final meal, then he might have chosen Yom Kippur, the Day of Atonement, instead of Passover. "But Passover suggests something more than forgiveness," he writes. "Passover marks the move from an old, slave existence to liberation. It is all about leaving an old land and entering a new one. It speaks of recreating a people, which is precisely what Jesus meant to do."[4]

Just as the Lord's Supper connects us to God's work of the past, it also points to another important meal of the future, the wedding supper of the Lamb, written about in Revelation 19:9: "Then the angel said to me, 'Write this: Blessed are those who are invited to the wedding supper of the Lamb!' And he added, 'These are the true words of God.'" In that supper, the church is the bride and Jesus the Lamb. This marriage for eternity is the fulfillment of all the other suppers, which can be seen as a rehearsal or foreshadowing of that great meal.

The Lord's Supper makes us hungry for that culminating meal that is to come. In the churches I have been part of over the years, people often poke fun at the little wafers we use for Communion, hard little discs stamped with a cross that hardly look edible at all, let alone like actual bread. The little squirt of grape juice in the tiny plastic cup doesn't bear too much resemblance to wine either. Some churches have tried to fix this problem in various ways, improving the quality of bread and cup or using real chunks of bread that people dip into a common cup. Those changes are fine with me, but I am also happy with the tiny cup and bread-like sliver that I have known since childhood. As a physical meal, it is certainly not satisfying. It leaves me wanting more. I think that's what Communion should do. This meal is important, but there is more to come.

Communion invites those who participate to look back at what God has done, look forward to what God will do, and look inward to examine our own lives. As Paul warns the Corinthians, "Everyone ought to examine themselves before they eat of the bread and drink from the cup. For those who eat and drink without discerning the body of Christ eat and drink judgment on themselves" (1 Corinthians 11:28–29). Communion asks the participant to look one other place, to Jesus himself, in gratitude for his sacrifice, in awe of his presence. One day we will eat supper with him as we celebrate a bright eternity.

When the Last Supper ended, the longest night of Jesus's life had only begun. He and his disciples left that upper room and walked to a garden called Gethsemane, where Jesus's torment would begin.

Agony at Gethsemane

When the Gethsemane portion of Jesus's final twenty-four hours comes to my mind, I see it not in a continuous narrative but in vivid, agonizing fragments. These moments are from the Bible, but when I read the verses, I am surprised by how brief the account is compared to how it plays in my mind.

I see Jesus face down on the ground. He lies there alone. He knows the horror that will shortly overtake him. The torture. The mockery. The pain. The abandonment. The death. He will bear the sins of the world. Does it have to happen? Is there no other way? "My Father, if it is possible, may this cup be taken from me," he prays in Matthew 26:39. He is human. He is divine. He appeals to the Father. He has already told his friends, who are a little ways off, sleeping rather than praying, "My soul is overwhelmed with sorrow to the point of death" (v. 38). Sweat like drops of blood fall to the ground. An angel comes to strengthen him. Jesus takes all this agony to the Father. That's what Gethsemane means to me: Jesus takes his pain to the Father.

Jesus pours out his sorrow to the Father, but he also knows he has a mission to fulfill. He ends his prayer by saying, "Yet not as I will, but as you will" (v. 39). When I am in deepest pain, Gethsemane speaks to me. Jesus preaches no sermons in that garden. He tells no parables. His actions are his teaching. He reaches his lowest point, and he falls on his face and prays to the Father.

I have studied dozens of paintings of Gethsemane. Many of them disappoint me. Many show a tranquil Jesus, often sitting up, leaning against a boulder, his face upturned and awash in a heavenly glow, his hands politely folded in a praying position. Sometimes the brightly lit angel hovers nearby. Those images might make a pretty painting, but that's not the scene I wish someone could capture. In my mind's painting, I see Jesus face down, sweaty. The angel hovers not like a decorative cherub but like a medical professional rendering aid.

Another element of the story that many of the paintings leave out is the disciples, but they were there. They were not at their best, nor had they done so well in the hours leading up to this one. As Jesus prayed, Judas was in the process of betraying him and would soon arrive with the soldiers who would arrest him. Peter had just finished bragging about how he would never disown Jesus, even though he would soon do just that. Earlier, Jesus had addressed their petty dispute over which of them would be considered the greatest. By the time Jesus took them to the garden at Gethsemane at the foot of the Mount of Olives, they had endured a long and eventful evening and were tired and troubled and not likely to be of much help to anyone. Given their track record of even the previous few hours, no one could have blamed Jesus if he had chosen to go alone to Gethsemane to pray. He had put up with enough from his disciples and had some of the most horrendous hours in history still to face. However, despite the disciples' flaws, Jesus still wanted them with him. That's what his kingdom is about—people loving and supporting and praying for one another. He took them to Gethsemane so they would pray for him while he poured out his own prayer to the Father.

He asked all of them to pray, but he took three of them—Peter, James, and John—even farther into the garden with him than the others. Their task was straightforward: wait and pray. What a privilege! To be asked by Jesus himself to pray for him on the most momentous night of his ministry. Instead, they fell asleep. Not once, not twice, but three times as Jesus kept coming back to them from his own prayer. These friends failed him. They were exhausted. Their spirits were willing, but their flesh was weak, as Jesus told them. Still, he didn't throw them out of the garden. He gave them three chances, but there was no fourth. By then, Judas had come to betray Jesus to the gang that would arrest him.

Finally, the disciples were fully awake. One of them even cut off the ear of the high priest's servant, but Jesus put a stop to that and healed the man. The final events, prophesied for generations, had now been set in motion, and Jesus would fulfill his role in them. He could have brought down legions of angels to end this scene if he chose to. Instead, he would see it through. The disciples would fail Jesus one more time in this garden of sorrow. The scene at Gethsemane ends this way: "Then everyone deserted him and fled" (Mark 14:50).

Gethsemane is about prayer, but it is not about prayer as a feel-good exercise. Prayer that night did not bring Jesus the result he preferred, nor did it bring him comfort. He walked away from it with only one thing: the determination to carry out the Father's will. Gethsemane shows that fellow believers will let us down, but we need them around us anyway. Jesus wanted his closest friends with him on that worst night, and even though they were too sleepy to pray as they should have, they came anyway. Their flawed presence was better than absence. Centuries later, the church is still flawed. It will let us down. It will frustrate us. But if we are to live in Jesus's kingdom as he intended, we don't have the luxury to give up on it. We need those fellow believers.

Jesus's disciples failed that night, but these men are also the ones who, several weeks later, would be at Pentecost when the Holy Spirit would come to start the work of the church. These men—and the new converts they would help bring into the movement—would build a church that would withstand hundreds of years of attempts to snuff it out. This church would survive in spite of constant assault by hostile dictators, armies, governments, competing religions, opposing philosophies, scandals, changing trends, epidemics of indifference, unsympathetic cultural, artistic, and entertainment forces, and countless other enemies. Gethsemane was not a proud moment for the disciples. But it was not the end.

Notes

1. Buzz Aldrin, "Guideposts Classics: Buzz Aldrin on Communion in Space," *Guideposts*, July 10, 2014, https://www.guideposts.org/better-living/life-advice/finding-life-purpose/guideposts-classics-buzz-aldrin-on-communion-in-space?nopaging=1.

2. Aldrin, "Communion in Space."

3. Henri J. M. Nouwen, *The Return of the Prodigal Son: A Story of Homecoming* (New York: Doubleday, 1992), 113.

4. Tim Stafford, *Surprised by Jesus: His Agenda for Changing Everything in A.D. 30 and Today* (Downers Grove, IL: IVP Books, 2006), 179.

Digging Deeper

1. Meals play an important role throughout the Bible. The Passover meal, the marriage supper of the Lamb, the wedding banquet of Jesus's parable, and many others are prominently featured. Why do you think meals are given such significance in the Bible? Why is the setting of a meal particularly appropriate for what Jesus wanted to accomplish on his last evening with his disciples?

2. In what ways does the Last Supper connect past, present, and future?

3. Jesus's sleepy disciples failed him as he prayed at Gethsemane, and once the soldiers showed up, the disciples fled. Why did Jesus want them with him anyway as he prayed his agonized prayer?

4. What does Jesus's time spent praying in Gethsemane teach us about the purpose and importance of prayer?

Go to https://www.thefoundrypublishing.com/12NT/LeaderGuide for a free downloadable leader's guide that includes more questions for reflection as well as activities for use in a small group setting.

12

Michelangelo's *Pieta* // Michelangelo // c. 1498-1499

The Cross

²² They brought Jesus to the place called Golgotha (which means "the place of the skull"). ²³ Then they offered him wine mixed with myrrh, but he did not take it. ²⁴ And they crucified him. Dividing up his clothes, they cast lots to see what each would get.

²⁵ It was nine in the morning when they crucified him. ²⁶ The written notice of the charge against him read: THE KING OF THE JEWS.

²⁷ They crucified two rebels with him, one on his right and one on his left. ²⁹ Those who passed by hurled insults at him, shaking their heads and saying, "So! You who are going to destroy the temple and build it in three days, ³⁰ come down from the cross and save yourself!" ³¹ In the same way the chief priests and the teachers of the law mocked him among themselves. "He saved others," they said, "but he can't save himself! ³² Let this Messiah, this king of Israel, come down now from the cross, that we may see and believe." Those crucified with him also heaped insults on him.

³³ At noon, darkness came over the whole land until three in the afternoon. ³⁴ And at three in the afternoon Jesus cried out in a loud voice, "Eloi, Eloi, lema sabachthani?" (which means "My God, my God, why have you forsaken me?").

³⁵ When some of those standing near heard this, they said, "Listen, he's calling Elijah."

³⁶ Someone ran, filled a sponge with wine vinegar, put it on a staff, and offered it to Jesus to drink. "Now leave him alone. Let's see if Elijah comes to take him down," he said.

³⁷ With a loud cry, Jesus breathed his last.

³⁸ The curtain of the temple was torn in two from top to bottom. ³⁹ And when the centurion, who stood there in front of Jesus, saw how he died, he said, "Surely this man was the Son of God!"

—Mark 15:22–39

IF YOU HAD to narrow down Christianity to one symbol, it would be the cross. It is a symbol recognized around the world, even by those who know little or nothing about the faith it represents. Few symbols of any kind have become so prevalent. If you looked hard enough, you could find billions of them around the world.

Start with the Hill of Crosses in Lithuania. On one hill, an estimated 200,000 crosses of every imaginable size and design have been planted by pilgrims coming to offer prayers or to memorialize the dead. Some of the crosses go back hundreds of years. When the Soviet Union controlled the area after World War II, it tried repeatedly to destroy the crosses. As Martin Gray explains, "Three times, during 1961, 1973, and 1975, the hill was leveled, the crosses were burned or turned into scrap metal, and the area was covered with waste and sewage. Following each of these desecrations local inhabitants and pilgrims from all over Lithuania rapidly replaced crosses upon the sacred hill."[1] The Soviets eventually gave up their determination to destroy the site, and Lithuania gained its independence in 1991. Now people from all over the world come to see the crosses or to carefully plant their own on the crowded hill.

Crosses loom above millions of churches around the world. Every second untold thousands of people are making the sign of the cross over their body. Giant crosses are constructed on hillsides and in fields in places around the world as a sign of devotion to Christ. In a small village called Tesqopa outside the city of Mosul in Iraq, a giant cross was erected in early 2017 to celebrate the removal of the Islamic State (or ISIS) terrorist group from the town. The Chaldean Catholic Patriarch of Baghdad, Louis Sako, said the cross was "the first spark of light shining in all the cities of the Nineveh plain since the darkness of ISIS, which lasted almost two and a half years."[2]

Half a world away, off Interstate 40 in the Texas panhandle, a large white cross rises 19 stories high from the flat landscape, visible for miles around. In Effingham, Illinois, people from many countries have come to visit what is billed as the world's largest cross, towering 198 feet tall. Victory Baptist Church in Henry County, Virginia, built their own huge cross that stands 110 feet high, with a top portion that weighs more than 30 tons. In Tomball, Texas, a mother erected a 125-foot cross to honor her son who died at the age of 25. I could give hundreds more examples of public crosses that have been built as a witness to the Christian faith.

People also display crosses in more personal and intimate ways, wearing them as jewelry or emblazoning them on their belongings. On one website alone, I found 6,679 different crosses to choose from. There were necklaces displaying every imaginable cross design, made from just about any material you could think of—gold, silver, stainless steel, cast iron, wood, and plastic. Some crosses were encrusted with jewels, some covered with colorful designs, some even sporting an American flag design. There were dog tags with crosses, cross-shaped lapel pins, bookmarks in the shape of a cross, ballpoint pens with clips shaped like a cross, wall crosses, crucifix statues, cross-decorated stationery, and many other products. Almost all of these crosses are made to be attractive. They're decorations. You can buy a cross for your wall with a frame for your family portrait in the middle of it.

It's easy to look at all of this commercialization of the cross and quickly conclude that it trivializes this important Christian symbol. In many cases, that is true. People may wear the necklaces or lapel pins only because they look nice, with no thought given to the excruciating and momentous event that happened on the actual cross that all these other crosses symbolize.

However, for many Christians these symbols—even though they look like nothing more than attractive wardrobe accessories—may be more meaningful to their spiritual lives than appearances would suggest. When a believer happens to place a hand on the cross hanging on a chain around his or her neck, the feel of that cross may at least occasionally be a reminder of Christ and of the believer's own Christian commitment. In times of stress or crisis, holding onto that cross may help bring clarity in prayer. The cross can also serve as a witness to others, a wordless message that says, "I belong to Christ. This is where I stand."

The public crosses, whether they are giant ones that can be seen for many miles, or smaller ones that grace the tops of church steeples, may also serve as a powerful witness or invitation to Jesus Christ. At the giant cross in Effingham, Illinois, for example, people leave prayers and other messages at the base. They feel drawn to it as it helps them connect or reconnect to their faith.

Of course, any symbol this powerful is also going to be abused or appropriated for purposes that do not represent Christ. A cross on top of a church means one thing. A cross burning on a lawn holds an entirely different and sinister meaning. A cross in a vampire movie may represent a wide range of things, from comedy to a kind of magic power to a somewhat twisted acknowledgement of the actual significance of the Christian faith and its spiritual battle with evil. Filmmakers or other artists who are hostile to Christianity can use the cross just as freely as Christians can, slapping a big cross around the neck of a hypocritical priest or church lady to emphasize the disconnect between what the religion teaches and how its adherents sometimes behave.

The cross has also been attacked throughout history, and even today, by governments and the legal process. Many crosses that have been erected or hung in public spaces have been challenged on legal grounds, and those who show or wear a cross in certain countries face persecution or death.

Still, no matter how much critics have tried to taint the cross's meaning or obliterate all that it stands for, believers still revere it. Besides church buildings and jewelry and an occasional cross on a hillside, another place where the cross makes a frequent appearance—millions of appearances, in fact—is in cemeteries. When Christians are laid to rest, they often want this important symbol on their tombstone to underscore the importance of their faith.

As I considered the cross's appearance on millions of graves around the world, I found a document from the U.S. Department of Veterans Affairs National Cemetery Administration that lists the religious emblems allowed on government headstones and markers. Symbols for many different religions are allowed, but what I learned about the cross surprised me. The government allows not only one or two designs for the cross on gravestones and markers but more than I knew even existed. There is the Latin cross, Presbyterian cross, Russian Orthodox cross, Lutheran cross, Episcopal cross, United Methodist cross, Serbian Orthodox cross, Greek cross, Christian Reformed Church cross, Christian & Missionary Alliance cross, and more than a dozen others.[3] Some designs were so creative that it was hard to even discern that they *were* crosses. But as long as these cemeteries exist, those graves will bear silent witness to the deceased person's faith in Jesus Christ.

The Cross of Jesus: What You Know, or Thought You Knew

The cross is now depicted in hundreds of ways, but what did the actual cross on which Jesus Christ was crucified look like? No one knows. Even though you may have seen the crucifixion portrayed so many times that you feel certain you must have read a description of it, significant portions of the event—such as the actual nailing of Jesus to the cross—are not described in any of the Gospel accounts. What was the shape and design of the cross? Was Jesus crucified on what is known as a Latin cross, with the crossbar a little above the middle of the vertical stake, as is often portrayed? Or was he crucified on a St. Anthony's cross, with the crossbeam at the *top* of the vertical stake? Robin Jensen, who wrote a book on the cross's history and impact, says that some "crosses" of that era were simply a single vertical post with the prisoner's hands nailed or tied above their heads.[4] Any of these are possibilities. The Gospel writers did not say.

What about the nails? Surely the Bible describes what so many Christians have pictured in their minds and seen acted out in films and Passion plays: the horrific sight of soldiers nailing Jesus's hands and feet to the cross. It isn't there. As Jensen points out, nails are never mentioned until after Jesus's resurrection, when Thomas—forever after known as Doubting Thomas—says to his fellow disciples, "Unless I see the nail marks in his hands and put my finger where the nails were, and put my hand into his side, I will not believe" (John 20:25).

Why did the Gospel writers not describe the details of the cross or crucifixion itself? Did they think their audience would already know how to picture it? Or did they believe no further emphasis needed to be directed toward this horrible and humiliating style of death? Many modern readers, with our fashionable cross necklaces and wall decorations, have tamed the torturous reality of the cross so much that it no longer sends chills through us the way, for instance, the details of death in a Nazi gas chamber might.

However, for those who lived in Jesus's day—including his closest followers—death on the cross was a shocking event. In Passion plays and other depictions, the crucifixion is often presented in such a stylized way that its brutality is inadvertently downplayed. Archaeologists uncovered a crucified man's right heel bone with a nail still piercing it from where it had been nailed to a cross. I saw a photograph of that nail-pierced heel bone, and even though it captured only a small portion of the reality of crucifixion, that image hit me harder than any church-pageant crucifixion I have ever seen because my mind couldn't help but imagine the force it must have taken to drive that spike through this person's bones—and the pain and terror the person must have suffered.

The execution of Jesus Christ on the cross has such enormous theological significance and such inherent dramatic intensity that it has been an irresistible subject matter for artists of nearly every genre. Painters have captured it on canvases for centuries, the church produced plays about it in the era when most Christians did not have the opportunity to read the story for themselves in the Bible, and directors have brought it to life on film repeatedly throughout the last hundred years. Passion plays have been popular for at least seven hundred years. In the fourteenth and fifteenth centuries, these performances could involve a couple hundred actors and capture the attention of entire cities in festivals centered on this event. One of the well-known Passion plays today is the one in Oberammergau in Bavaria, Germany. It started in 1634 and is performed every ten years in that village.[5] Many churches now produce their own Passion plays as part of their Easter celebrations.

Painters of every era have also been eager to provide their own interpretation of that momentous day when Jesus hung on a cross between two criminals. Some of the famous painters who have chosen the crucifixion of Christ as their subject matter over the centuries include Fra Angelica, Gerard David, Hieronymus Bosch, Raphael, Rembrandt, Peter Paul Rubens, Tintoretto, El Greco, Gustave Dore, Paul Gauguin, Pablo Picasso, Salvador Dali, and many others. The diversity of that list of artists is indicative of the variety of portrayals of the event in these artists' works.

Some realistically emphasize the physical agony Jesus suffers, while others stay away from realism altogether, showing him surrounded by haloed saints or depicting the scene in more abstract or stylized ways. Some set the crucifixion in a place that looks more like the artist's own country than a Middle Eastern landscape, with onlookers wearing clothes that fit the period in which they were painted rather than garments of the first century. Some paintings approach the crucifixion devotionally, with a sense of reverence and awe, while others treat it historically at best, if not ironically. No matter what the attitude or approach of the artist, none of them can resist the drama and significance of this supremely important historical event.

If the death of Jesus on the cross fascinated painters and Passion play authors for centuries, then it is no surprise that, when film came along, moviemakers felt compelled to recreate the event too. The crucifixion has been depicted in every era of film. Among the more famous film depictions, Cecil B. DeMille portrayed it in *King of Kings* in 1927, Henry Koster in *The Robe* in 1953, William Wyler in *Ben-Hur* in 1959, George Stevens in *The Greatest Story Ever Told* in 1965, Norman Jewison in *Jesus Christ, Superstar* in 1973, Franco Zefferelli in *Jesus of Nazareth* in 1977, Martin Scorsese in *The Last Temptation of Christ* in 1988, and Mel Gibson in *The Passion of the Christ* in 2004.[6] Dozens of others could be mentioned. Like the painters, the filmmakers treat the event with every imaginable perspective, from reverence to satire to blasphemy.

Since the story has already been told so many times, why do artists and filmmakers feel inspired to tell it yet again? One of the most well-known recent retellings of the story of Christ on the cross is Mel Gibson's *The Passion of the Christ*. Before directing this film, Gibson was better known for starring in movies such as *Lethal Weapon, Mad Max, Hamlet, Braveheart*, and others. He is a controversial celebrity who has had brushes with scandal. But he felt he had to tell this story. In a foreword to a companion book to the film, Gibson says that the movie had its genesis during a time when he found himself "trapped with feelings of terrible, isolated emptiness." He turned to God in prayer. Once the idea for the movie came to him, he looked at some of the famous paintings of the Passion story. Staying close to Scripture, he says he "wanted the effort to be a testament to the infinite love of Jesus Christ, which has saved, and continues to save, many the world over." Like many others who have depicted these events in various artistic modes across the centuries, Gibson hoped that his film would "help many more people recognize the power of [God's] love."[7]

The Scandal of the Cross

Films like *The Passion of the Christ* depict the brutality and horror of the cross in ways that even the biblical writers themselves did not dwell on. One element that many of the representations of Christ's crucifixion—whether on canvas, stage, or film—have had in common over the centuries is that they imbue Christ's suffering with a sense of nobility and significance. That makes sense, considering the fact that Christians believe Christ's death on the cross made possible our own eternal salvation. By now the cross, for many, has such a stained-glass-window exaltedness to it—or else a department-store-jewelry triviality to it—that it is hard to see the scandal that the first Christians and nonbelievers of that era would have seen.

For many people at the time of Jesus's execution, and for a long time after, until familiarity with the story helped perceptions to change, death on a cross was an embarrassing, humiliating way to die. It was appropriate only for vile criminals. If Jesus was God, how could he possibly die in such a crude and vulgar way? How would his followers ever explain it? How could they embrace it?

Robin Jensen explains that "Jews, awaiting a kingly messiah, saw death by crucifixion as cursed and contradictory to their expectations; pagans could not fathom a crucified god. The former found it incomprehensible, the latter ludicrous."[8] Like so much else in Christianity—love your enemies, pray for those who persecute you—the cross turns people's expectations upside down. If the Savior had to die at all, the horror of the cross would certainly seem like an inappropriate method. No wonder Jesus's original followers had trouble understanding or accepting it.

As commentator Fleming Rutledge notes, the significance of Jesus's death on the cross is not apparent simply from the action itself. It has to be interpreted.[9] Jesus was arrested, dragged away, tortured, and killed on a cross. Although Jesus had done some preparation for his disciples for what was about to happen, on the day of the event itself, no one was there to give a running commentary to the disciples or other onlookers about the theological significance of the events that were taking place. Coming to terms with the meaning of the death came later, after Jesus's resurrection, the coming of the Holy Spirit at Pentecost, the preaching of Paul and others, and the church's working out of its own theology in the generations that followed.

In preaching Christianity to the world in those early days, Paul knew the cross was a difficult but crucial element for his audience to understand. In 1 Corinthians he says that "we preach Christ crucified: a stumbling block to Jews and foolishness to Gentiles" (1:23). The death of Christ is at the center of Christianity, but as Paul and other early followers knew, it was also the strangest part of the faith. Rutledge says, "Christianity is unique. The world's religions have certain traits in common, but until the gospel of Jesus Christ burst upon the Mediterranean world, no one in the history of human imagination had conceived of such a thing as the worship of a crucified man."[10] By admitting that the crucifixion is foolishness to the Greeks (the gentiles) and a stumbling block to Jews, Paul acknowledges that this bizarre aspect of Christianity won't make sense to those outside the faith, "but to those whom God has called, both Jews and Greeks, Christ the power of God and the wisdom of God. For the foolishness of God is wiser than human wisdom, and the weakness of God is stronger than human strength" (vv. 24–25).

The execution of a movement's leader in many cases would mean the end of the movement. Christianity might have ended with Jesus's death. Instead, the importance of his sacrifice puts it at the center of the faith. Paul puts it succinctly in 1 Corinthians 15:3–4: "For what I received I passed on to you as of first importance: that Christ died for our sins according to the Scriptures, that he was buried, that he was raised on the third day according to the Scriptures." Paul, along with other biblical writers and countless theologians across the centuries, has written further explanations of how Christ's sacrificial death covers our sins and makes us right with God, but the central truth of the gospel is that it *does*, and that believing in him is the way to salvation and eternal life. When we believe and put our trust in Jesus Christ, we believe that our sins were crucified on that cross.

The cross continues to have meaning for believers as we identify with Christ and his suffering. Christians do not simply *observe* the crucifixion as bystanders. In Galatians Paul says, "I have been crucified with Christ and I no longer live, but Christ lives in me" (2:20). Christ died for us, but we also die with him. Becoming a Christian is a kind of crucifixion. We let the old life die. We become one with Christ. For Christians, the response to Christ's death on the cross is not *only* gratitude. It is also *participation*. We let who we used to be die so that Christ may fill up the new life that replaces the old.

What does it mean to be crucified with Christ? Commentator John Barnts points out that Jesus often identifies directly with his followers. For example, in Matthew 25:40, Jesus says, "Whatever you did for one of the least of these brothers and sisters of mine, you did for me," and during Paul's conversion experience on the road to Damascus, Jesus asks him, "Why do you persecute me?" Jesus doesn't accuse him of persecuting his followers but of persecuting *him*. He is one with his followers. Barnts adds, "No one looks at a grapevine and says, 'Hey, look at that vine. Oh, and look at those branches!' Same with a human body. We see a person, not some head attached to some body, as if they hardly belong together."[11] If we are united in that way with Christ then, as Romans 8 showed us, we are united in his suffering as well as in the promise of eternal life to come.

The cross—whether we wear it on a decorative chain around our neck or hang it on a wall or simply carry its image in our minds—can symbolize that powerful, mysterious connection to our Savior. The cross was a crucial element in Jesus's story, but thankfully, it was not the end of his story. Three days after his execution on that wooden death device, Jesus would shake the world once again.

Notes

1. Martin Gray, "Hill of Crosses," *Places of Peace and Power*, https://sacredsites.com/europe/lithuania/hill_of_crosses.html.

2. Anugrah Kumar, "Christians Erect Giant Cross Outside Mosul to Mark Victory Over ISIS Jihadists," *The Christian Post*, February 26, 2017, https://www.christianpost.com/news/christians-erect-giant-cross-mosul-mark-victory-isis-jihadists-islamic-state-175936/.

3. "Available Emblems of Belief for Placement on Government Headstones and Markers," U.S. Department of Veterans Affairs, National Cemetery Administration, https://www.cem.va.gov/cem/hmm/emblems.asp.

4. Robin M. Jensen, *The Cross: History, Art, and Controversy*, (Cambridge, MA: Harvard University Press, 2017), 9.

5. "Passion play," *New World Encyclopedia*, http://www.newworldencyclopedia.org/entry/Passion_play.

6. Peter T. Chattaway, "History and Tradition in Movie Depictions of the Cross," *Film-Chat* (blog), April 8, 2013, https://www.patheos.com/blogs/filmchat/2013/04/history-and-tradition-in-movie-depictions-of-the-cross.html.

7. Mel Gibson and Ken Duncan, *The Passion: Photography from the Movie "The Passion of the Christ"* (Wheaton, IL: Tyndale House Publishers, 2004).

8. Jensen, *The Cross,* 2.

9. Fleming Rutledge, *The Crucifixion: Understanding the Death of Jesus Christ* (Grand Rapids, MI: Eerdmans, 2015), 8.

10. Ibid., 1.

11. John Barnts, "Crucified with Christ?" *Barnts in the Belfry* (blog), April 12, 2017, https://barntsinthebelfry.wordpress.com/2017/04/12/crucified-with-christ/.

Digging Deeper

1. Of all the symbols that could represent Christianity, why do you think the cross has emerged as the central symbol? Why do people wear it as jewelry or build giant crosses along the highway?

2. This chapter points out that, at the time of Jesus's crucifixion, death on a cross was equated with scandal. Paul called it "a stumbling block to Jews and foolishness to Gentiles" (1 Corinthians 1:23). Of all the ways Jesus could have been killed, what is the significance of the fact that he was executed in this horrible way, on a cross?

3. Jesus's crucifixion has been depicted in Passion plays, paintings, and films. What is the most powerful depiction of this event that you have seen? What was it about that portrayal that made it so meaningful?

Go to https://www.thefoundrypublishing.com/12NT/LeaderGuide for a free downloadable leader's guide that includes more questions for reflection as well as activities for use in a small group setting.

13

A tomb near Nazareth // Mordechai Meiri

The Resurrection

¹ *After the Sabbath, at dawn on the first day of the week, Mary Magdalene and the other Mary went to look at the tomb.*

² *There was a violent earthquake, for an angel of the Lord came down from heaven and, going to the tomb, rolled back the stone and sat on it.* ³ *His appearance was like lightning, and his clothes were white as snow. The guards were so afraid of him that they shook and became like dead men.*

⁵ *The angel said to the women, "Do not be afraid, for I know that you are looking for Jesus, who was crucified.* ⁶ *He is not here; he has risen, just as he said. Come and see the place where he lay.* ⁷ *Then go quickly and tell his disciples: 'He has risen from the dead and is going ahead of you into Galilee. There you will see him.' Now I have told you."*

⁸ *So the women hurried away from the tomb, afraid yet filled with joy, and ran to tell his disciples.* ⁹ *Suddenly Jesus met them. "Greetings," he said. They came to him, clasped his feet and worshiped him.* ¹⁰ *Then Jesus said to them, "Do not be afraid. Go and tell my brothers to go to Galilee; there they will see me."*

—*Matthew 28:1–10*

JESUS CHRIST rose from the dead.

That fact makes all the difference. Without it, Christianity crumbles and Jesus becomes just another disappointment, a wannabe messiah who wasn't the real thing at all. Even a false messiah could die, but only a real one could rise from the dead. Jesus Christ rose from the dead. Afterward, he appeared to many people on multiple occasions before his ascension to the Father. They saw him. They touched him. They talked to him.

The importance of this historical event cannot be overstated, but we also cannot make sense of it outside the context of what else happened during those extraordinary days and beyond. Lazarus also rose from the dead, for instance, but his resurrection was not central to our faith. It's not just the coming back to life of a formerly dead person that matters. It's what Jesus's resurrection accomplishes. When he ascended to the Father, as Acts 1:9–10 describes, his sacrifice for our sins was complete and accepted by the Father. Jesus is now there before the Father, interceding for us as our advocate. As Hebrews 9:24 tells us, "For Christ did not enter a sanctuary made with human hands that was only a copy of the true one; he entered heaven itself, now to appear for us in God's presence."

Jesus lives with the Father, but there is even more to the story than that. As Mark Galli puts it, "the great miracle that the gospel proclaims is not merely that Christ lived bodily after the crucifixion but that he lives dynamically in us today."[1] Galli notes that Paul uses the phrase that we are "in Christ" more than two hundred times. Paul also says that Christ is in us: "And if anyone does not have the Spirit of Christ, they do not belong to Christ. But if Christ is in you, then even though your body is subject to death because of sin, the Spirit gives life because of righteousness" (Romans 8:9b–10). We often speak of receiving the Holy Spirit, but Galli explains that part of the "mystery of the Trinity" is that, because of the unity of the Trinity, "we can also understand why Paul sometimes says we are indwelt by the 'Spirit of Christ.'"[2]

Given the enormous importance of Jesus's resurrection in the history of the world and in the theology of the Christian faith, it's tempting to talk about it in the grandiose terms it deserves and simply leave it at that. But there is another side to Jesus's resurrection. When he rose from the dead after lying in the tomb for three days, look at how he did it. It was not a public event. There was no fanfare. It was very different from the Pentecost event that would happen weeks later. At Pentecost, the Holy Spirit would arrive in a crowded room, with tongues of fire and the miracle of languages. There was preaching, baptism, and the conversion of more than three thousand people, and the celebratory launching of the church.

The resurrection of Jesus Christ happened much more quietly. There was an earthquake when the angel rolled away the stone from the tomb, but only a few people were there to experience it. There was no public rally with lights and music and a dramatic, triumphant appearance of Jesus. He appeared to his disciples many times in the following days, but when he did so, he came to small, intimate gatherings of friends. He ate and drank and listened and talked. He readied them for the coming of the Holy Spirit and for his own ascension. He was only there for a little while, and not for spectacle. He was showing them that he was alive, and he was establishing many witnesses to that fact, but he would not be there long. He would ascend to the Father, and the next phase of the church would begin at Pentecost. A triumphal, spectacular return would happen eventually, but this was not the time.

My favorite stories of the aftermath of Jesus's resurrection were the times when he showed up unexpectedly and caught people by surprise so much that they didn't even recognize him at first. On the day Jesus rose from the dead, some of his followers were walking to a village called Emmaus not far from Jerusalem. Jesus joined two of them on their walk, but he didn't reveal his identity. He asked them what they were talking about, and they told him the story of Jesus, a prophet they had hoped would redeem Israel but who had been crucified instead. And now, three days later, some of the women had reported that Jesus's tomb was empty and that angels had appeared to them and told them he was alive. What could it mean?

Jesus planted a few strong hints by reminding them about the prophecies that indicated the Messiah would have to go through the kind of suffering the man they are talking about experienced. When they reached the village, Jesus was about to go on, but they urged him to come and spend more time with them. He did so. They sat down for a meal together, and once he took bread, gave thanks for it, and gave it to them, "their eyes were opened and they recognized him, and he disappeared from their sight. They asked each other, 'Were not our hearts burning within us while he talked with us on the road and opened the Scriptures to us?'" (Luke 24:31-32).

I love the fact that this is how the resurrected Jesus made himself known to them—by walking with them, talking to them and listening to their story, teaching them, accepting their invitation to spend more time with them, praying with them, and breaking bread with them. The burning inside them—like the tongues of fire that will come by the Holy Spirit on Pentecost—lets them know they are with the Messiah. This is how Jesus, through the Holy Spirit and through his presence among other Christians, still makes himself known today. How many of us have been drawn to him by that same kind of burning within ourselves, that same relationship that draws us to him?

Jesus rose from the dead. We can know him. Jesus's resurrection was physical. He was not simply a spirit floating around. It is no accident that when he meets with people after rising from the dead, he often eats and drinks with them. The great hope for us is that our own resurrection in eternity will also be in a body. Jesus's resurrection is a foreshadowing of our own. Paul expounds on this reality throughout 1 Corinthians 15. He calls Jesus the "firstfruits" of those who have died and been resurrected. He says, "For as in Adam all die, so in Christ all will be made alive. But each in turn: Christ, the firstfruits; then, when he comes, those who belong to him" (vv. 22-23). Or, as Tim Stafford puts it, "Jesus's resurrection is the first installment of total resurrection. . . . We are body-persons—always have been, always will be. Jesus's resurrection leads the way for body life eternally. The tide has turned. The victory is won. The wonderful creation will be cleansed and completed, with pain and death wiped away."[3]

The primary symbol of Christianity is the cross. That is not surprising, since the crucifixion of Jesus Christ plays a critical role in the history and theology of this faith and the history of the world. But I wish there were an equally powerful symbol for the resurrection of Christ. His resurrection is just as crucial as his crucifixion. No symbol captures it. I have seen pictures of an empty tomb, but symbolically they lack the simplicity and force of a symbol like a cross.

The resurrection does have its own holiday in the Christian calendar, Easter. But if you were to ask most people what symbol first comes to mind when they think of Easter, you would probably be as likely to get a pagan symbol as a Christian one. Easter eggs, they might say. Or an Easter bunny. Or an Easter basket. Easter has not been commercialized to quite the radical extent that Christmas has, but it is still a big business. In the United States alone, according to the National Retail Federation, Easter is a $17-billion-a-year holiday. Americans color more than 18 million eggs and buy 43 million cards, 90 million chocolate bunnies, 500 million Cadbury Creme eggs, and 700 million Peeps each year.[4]

I must admit that my own personal behavior has helped boost each of those statistics, but chocolate bunnies and Peeps have played no role in helping me understand or celebrate the resurrection of Christ. As with Christmas, Christians have long been happy to mix religious and nonreligious elements as we celebrate our Christian holidays. The origin of the term "Easter" itself has sometimes been attributed not to Christian sources but to a German goddess of fertility. And what of Easter bunnies? Rabbits have also served as symbols of fertility, and the Easter bunny tradition is often linked to German immigrants of the 1700s who "transported their tradition of an egg-laying hare called Osterhase or *Oschter Haws*. Their children made nests in which this creature could lay its colored eggs."[5] Some Easter traditions have possible connections to Jesus's resurrection that are tenuous at best. Eggs may represent new life, as Jesus's rising from the dead represents new life. That may have helped the Easter egg tradition catch on, and that tradition may be connected to the popularity of a particularly egg-shaped candy, the jelly bean. More than 16 billion of those little treats are produced each Easter.[6]

When I was growing up, it was common for people to dress up for Easter and buy new outfits for the whole family. Maybe that tradition was somehow tied to the newness of life that the resurrection represents, or maybe it was just an excuse to get a new outfit for spring, or maybe a little of both. One way of looking at Easter traditions like chocolate bunnies and Easter baskets is that, like some of the nonreligious elements of Christmas, they do at least bring a sense of joy and celebration to these holidays. Families gather. Gifts are given. Delicious food is eaten. Kids get excited. Church celebrations have a heightened sense of significance and wonder. But, just as Jesus sometimes gets drowned out of Christmas by the commercialized emphasis on gift-buying and elaborate decorating and frantic schedules, Jesus is also easily pushed out of Easter by bunnies and eggs. I personally don't want to get rid of any of the traditions, which I enjoy, but I wish there were more ways to make people's first thoughts of Easter more about Jesus's resurrection than about Peeps.

Experiencing Jesus's Story As If You Have Never Heard It

The events stretching from the Last Supper to the Resurrection take up three chapters in Matthew, three in Mark, three in Luke, and eight in John. That is not a huge portion of the Bible as a whole, but those chapters form a large part of people's perception of the Christian story. Ask someone for an image that comes to mind when they think of Christianity, and you're likely to get something from one of those chapters. Jesus on the cross. Jesus offering the bread and the cup. Nail-scarred hands. Empty tomb.

I wish we could see the story anew. Many of us cannot remember a time in our lives when we didn't know the whole story. We can't remember reading about the crucifixion without already knowing that three days later Jesus would rise from the dead. I wish we had the power *not* to know, in order to experience the joy of it, the miracle of it, with the same sense of wonder and edge-of-our-seat tension we feel when we're watching a suspenseful movie for the first time or reading an expertly paced novel.

Familiarity can make us grow complacent even about the most consequential story ever told. I invite you to ask the Lord to let you experience the story again with its full force. I invite you to prayerfully pick up one of the Gospels again and read those culminating chapters straight through as if you have never heard the story before. The final week of Jesus's life on earth turned civilization upside down, and it has the power to change you too.

Notes

1. Mark Galli, "The Most Astonishing Easter Miracle," *Christianity Today*, April 2017, 31.

2. Galli, "Easter Miracle," 32.

3. Tim Stafford, *Surprised by Jesus: His Agenda for Changing Everything in A.D. 30 and Today* (Downers Grove, IL: IVP Books, 2006), 218.

4. Danny Cox, "Easter 2016 by the Numbers: Peeps, Chocolate Bunnies, Eggs, and Money—How Much Is Eaten and Spent?" *Inquisitr*, March 26, 2016, https://www.inquisitr .com/2929316/easter-2016-by-the-numbers-peeps-chocolate-bunnies-eggs-and-money-how -much-is-eaten-and-spent/.

5. "Easter Symbols and Traditions," *History*, n.d., https://www.history.com/topics/holidays /easter-symbols.

6. "Easter Symbols and Traditions," *History*.

Digging Deeper

1. These chapters focusing on the Last Supper, Gethsemane, the cross, and the resurrection of Jesus Christ have brought to mind the most significant events in Christian history. If you could have been present for only one of those events, what would it be, and why?

2. For many people, Easter—if they celebrate it at all—has become more about chocolate bunnies, Easter eggs, and Peeps than about Jesus's resurrection. If you were in charge of Easter, what would you do to put the focus back on Christ?

3. The Last Supper is represented by the bread and the cup. Christ's crucifixion is powerfully symbolized by the cross. The resurrection lacks such a well-known symbol. What do you think that symbol should be?

Go to https://www.thefoundrypublishing.com/12NT/LeaderGuide for a free downloadable leader's guide that includes more questions for reflection as well as activities for use in a small group setting.

14

Photo by Lincoln Rogers

No Force Can Stop the Bible—Except One

PEOPLE HAVE DIED to get the Bible into your hands.

Throughout the last two thousand years, a remarkable combination of technological, historical, and theological forces have conspired to move the Bible from being a rare document in the hands of only a few people to a book available to billions of people in hundreds of languages.

One thread that runs through the history of the Bible is the impulse to get the Word out there, no matter the barriers or the cost. In eras when people did not have the ability to read it for themselves, or when technology limited the number of copies that could be distributed, dramatists found ways to present the Bible stories in plays, and artists found ways to vividly show them in paintings and sculptures. When governments or church officials showed hostility toward getting the Bible into people's hands in a language they could understand, brave translators defied them and created those Bibles anyway. Sometimes it cost them their lives.

Translators are still dying for this cause. In March 2016, four translators who worked for Wycliffe Associates in the Middle East were murdered to prevent them from working on the Bible. Militants also injured several other people in the attack and destroyed equipment and burned books and other translation material.[1] Such hostility to translation would have been familiar to the man the translation organization is named after, John Wycliffe. His belief that people should be able to read the Bible in their own language led to the first serious project to translate the entire Bible into English in the late 1300s. He was condemned for his view and his efforts and lost his position at Oxford University, but his followers brought that English translation into being.[2]

Church authorities condemned Wycliffe's Bible, but they couldn't stop it. Neither could anyone stop other English translations that followed, even though they tried. By the time William Tyndale came along in the 1500s, new printing technology brought great promise for widespread distribution of the Bible and other books, but church opposition still remained. Tyndale translated and printed his Bibles outside of England, and then they were brought into the country illegally. Although their distribution was widespread, the risks of supporting Tyndale or his Bible were great. As Bible historian Harry Freedman explains, "No one with a connection to Tyndale or his translation was safe. Thomas Hitton, a priest who had met Tyndale in Europe, confessed to smuggling two copies of the Bible into the country. He was charged with heresy and burnt alive. Thomas Bilney, a lawyer whose connection to Tyndale was tangential at most, was also thrown into the flames."[3] Other supporters were tortured or put in prison. Tyndale himself was burned at the stake in 1536.

People like Wycliffe and Tyndale are now famous because of their courageous actions to get the Bible into the hands of individuals, but hundreds of other translators and Bible smugglers whose names you will never know have also devoted years of their lives and faced enormous risks to spread this book throughout the world.

I believe the Bible is unstoppable. I believe that if any power were strong enough to snuff it out, that would have happened already. For every ominous development that indicates the Bible may be under threat or losing its relevance to a particular group of people, I can find another sign that gives me hope that the Bible is gaining new readers. For example, in 2017, the Museum of the Bible opened in Washington, DC. Prominently placed in the midst of the other great museums of the nation's capital, this museum tells the story of the Bible's influence across the centuries. Among the thousands of square feet of exhibits are rare Bibles from various eras, interactive exhibits that celebrate the Bible, and displays that show the Bible's cultural influence in music, civil rights, art, and film. There has never been a museum quite like it anywhere in the world. The Museum of the Bible also has a Scholars Initiative to promote research of the Bible. It also offers a Bible curriculum for those who want to study and teach the book. The museum has the potential to whet people's appetites for Scripture and lead them to delve more deeply into it.

The creation of a museum that celebrates the Bible is a hopeful sign, but I could match it with a discouraging one. *Christianity Today* reported on a Barna study that showed that, even though the Bible is still the most-read book in the world, the number of American adults who read it at least once a week dropped from 45 percent in 2009 to 33 percent in 2016. During that same seven-year period, the number of Americans who don't consider *any* book sacred—whether the Bible, the Koran, the Torah, or the Book of Mormon—doubled from 7 percent to 14 percent, with the biggest increase coming from people in their twenties and thirties.[4]

The article reports that, in order to bring the Bible to more people in that twenty-something generation, churches are trying everything they can think of, including digital tools such as "Bible apps, daily reading plans, study resources, podcasts, YouTube channels, plus more digital magazines, blogs, and websites than one can count." Some of those efforts seem to be paying off, with the online study resource Bible Hub reporting about 17 million page views and 1.7 million unique visitors per month among 18–34-year-olds, and BibleGateway drawing 30 percent of its audience from that generation.[5] Churches are also finding ways to foster relationships and personal connections among people of this generation—both online and in person—as a prelude to experiencing the Bible together.

Although I believe the Bible is unstoppable in a global sense, when it comes to how individuals treat it, it certainly can be stopped by one simple force: apathy. As an American literature professor, I know the danger of that one force to keep people from experiencing the depth of inspiration, pleasure, intellectual challenge, and sometimes even life transformation that great literature has to offer. I have never had a student seriously study literature and then say they regretted it or that it was a waste of time. My class can open the door to writers the students might otherwise never think to read: Thomas Wolfe, Edith Wharton, William Faulkner, Ralph Ellison, Emily Dickinson, and hundreds of others. The selection is rich, and we only touch the surface of the profound and entertaining literature that is available. When the course does what I hope it will, students walk away inspired by what they read and eager to read more on their own.

Some of the works we study—including classics like *The Adventures of Huckleberry Finn*—have been on banned-book lists of one kind or another, and some (including *Huck*) are still on some of those lists. Some works we study—such as Kate Chopin's *The Awakening* or Sarah Winnemucca's *Life Among the Paiutes*—were ignored by scholars and teachers for decades. Those outside forces, however, are not what keep students today from enjoying these authors. All this writing is readily available in our textbooks. The only force that can keep students away from this wealth of literature today is their own decision not to engage with it. A literary feast is laid before them, but some may simply choose to ignore it.

The same is true of the Bible. Persecution, execution, illiteracy, poor technology, and other forces have failed to stop the spread of Scripture. Motivated readers found ways around all those barriers in order to let the Word of God pour over them. But today, many readers are drowning in an ocean of Bibles—on their phones, their computers, in libraries, on their own bookshelves, in their churches, and elsewhere—yet they never touch it. Or, if they do, they treat it only as a spiritual snack, tasting a few crumbs of verses here or there but avoiding full meals. Like students in a literature class who don't do the reading, these Bible avoiders don't know what they're missing, but hope is not lost for them. At any time they can come to the table and dine, but many choose to go hungry instead.

When I was a young boy, I went through a phase in which I was a very picky eater. I liked only a few foods and refused to try any others. I can vaguely remember this. My family would get pizza, but all I wanted was crackers. I didn't like vegetables or fruit or meat. My mother became so concerned with my pickiness that she took me to the doctor. I don't know how a doctor would handle that today, but my doctor said, "Don't worry about it. When he gets hungry, he'll eat." The doctor was right. I don't remember what exactly made me start to try the foods that I ended up loving, but once I finally figured out that food like pizza, steak, corn, apples, bananas, burritos, and many others were actually delicious, I never again had to be coaxed to eat them. I was eager to do so, and now my challenge is quite the opposite, to try to keep from eating too many of them. I look back and wonder, how could I ever have voluntarily passed up pizza? So it is with Scripture. Once you have *really* tasted it, you will wonder why you ignored it for so long. Of course the Bible, like American literature, does not always reveal its benefits as readily as pizza does. Pizza is easy to enjoy. The Bible takes work, just as many of the other most meaningful experiences of life do.

One thing many people misunderstand about the Bible is that it cannot be reduced to the information it contains. It is possible to read it for the beauty of its poetry, the lessons of its stories, the impact of its theology, the legacy of its history, the majesty of its prophecies, the inspiration of its maxims, and the guidance of its principles. I would not discount the value of any of those motivations for reading Scripture, but I would add one more element that keeps bringing me back to the Bible: the Holy Spirit speaks through it. In ways that cannot be reduced to a simple summary of its contents, the Bible can bring us into the presence of God. When you are in someone's presence, such as when you go to a friend's home to have dinner, the worth of that experience cannot be reduced to only the words the person speaks. You want to be with the person. You certainly want to hear what they have to say, but if you were told that the meal would be canceled and you would be given merely a transcript of what the person had wanted to say, you would feel cheated. Words are an important part of a relationship with someone, but you want to experience the words through that person's presence. That can happen with the Bible. As you read it, as you let it flow into you, you gradually begin to know the God behind it.

The Bible opens up in many ways. Right this minute hundreds of biblical scholars are poring over thousands of the tiniest details of facts and interpretation. English professors are probing its literary techniques, as I have done in a Literature and the Bible course at my university. Pastors are illuminating it with their sermons. Bible studies are revealing its layers of meaning. Individual readers are launching into read-the-Bible-in-a-year studies, while other people are stumbling across forgotten Bibles on dusty shelves or in hotel drawers and picking it up and opening it for the first time.

Sometimes the Bible shows up in people's lives almost miraculously, as the Holy Spirit puts it in their paths. When I researched my book *God in Pursuit*, I found many stories of unusual or even bizarre ways that God used the Bible to draw people to him. For example, before his conversion, Charles G. Finney—who would become one of the greatest preachers of the nineteenth century—struggled in prayer under the weight of sin he felt. A portion of Scripture he wasn't even aware he knew and that he doesn't think he had ever *read* dropped into his mind "with a flood of light": "Then shall ye . . . go and pray unto me, and I will hearken unto you. And ye shall seek me, and find me, when ye shall search for me with all your heart" (Jeremiah 29:12-13, KJV). As he prayed through the rest of that day and into the night, more verses from the Bible kept flooding his mind. Finney says that he "seized hold of them, appropriated them, and fastened upon them with the grasp of a drowning man." Before the night was over, he had turned himself over to Christ.[6]

It is no accident that the Bible is the bestselling book of all time and that no power has been able to stop it. It is not a magic book. There is no shortcut to experiencing what it has to offer. It has inspired writers, artists, playwrights, poets, and musicians, but it has also been ignored by millions who scoffed at it or couldn't be bothered to read it. It has brought life and hope to millions, but it is up to you to decide what it will mean to you. Will you let it sit on a shelf, or will you open its pages and let it speak?

Notes

1. Sarah Eekhoff Zylstra, "Why Four Bible Translators Martyred in the Middle East Won't Be the Last," *Christianity Today*, March 24, 2016, https://www.christianitytoday.com/ct/channel/utilities/print.html?type=article&id=134038.

2. Harry Freedman, "The Murderous History of Bible Translations," *History Extra*, July 7, 2016, https://www.historyextra.com/period/medieval/the-murderous-history-of-bible-translations/.

3. Freedman, "The Murderous History of Bible Translators."

4. Cara Meredith, "Reaching a New Generation with the Bible," *Christianity Today*, August 1, 2017, https://www.christianitytoday.com/pastors/2017/bible-engagement/reaching-new-generation-with-bible.html.

5. Meredith, "Reaching a New Generation."

6. Quoted in Joseph Bentz, *God in Pursuit: The Tipping Points from Doubt to Faith* (Kansas City, MO: Beacon Hill Press of Kansas City, 2010), 94.

Acknowledgments

Completing this book would not have been possible without the support of friends and family who encouraged me, prayed for me, put up with me, advised me, and loved me. It will not be possible to mention by name everyone who has done one or more of those things for me, but I hope they know I am grateful.

I want to thank my wife, Peggy, for all her love and support of me and my writing. She keeps me centered and confident, and she also helpfully reads my early drafts. I am also grateful for the ongoing love of my other family members, particularly my children, Jacob and Katie. I would also like to thank my dad and my sister, Debbie.

Azusa Pacific University is a great place to work, and I appreciate their support of my writing over the years. I would especially like to thank my former department chair, David Esselstrom, and my current department chair, Windy Petrie. I am also grateful to the APU administration for their support and encouragement. My friends and students in the English Department have also been a source of help and inspiration to me.

I draw great strength from the Ninos, my Christian writers and artists prayer group that has prayed for every one of my books over the past twenty years. It is hard to imagine being a writer without their support. I am also grateful to my church and my pastor, Mike Platter. I am privileged to teach the Spectrum class there, and the friendship and ideas that have flowed from that experience are invaluable.

Steve Laube is my long-time agent and a steady source of wisdom and help.

Finally, I am grateful for Bonnie Perry, Audra Spiven, and the excellent editors and staff at The Foundry Publishing.

About the Author

Joseph Bentz, PhD, MA, is the author of *Nothing Is Wasted* (2016, available at thefoundrypublishing.com), and five other books on Christian living. He is also the author of four novels. Bentz is professor of American literature at Azusa Pacific University in Azusa, California, where he also serves as a faculty fellow in the university's Honors College and directs the Alpha Chi National Honor Society. He speaks and teaches nationwide. Bentz lives with his wife and two children in southern California. More information about his books and speaking is available at his website, josephbentz.com.